CHOOSING

A BIBLIO-

GRAPHIC

LESLIE R. MORRIS

UTILITY

Neal-Schuman Publishers, Inc.

New York

Published by Neal-Schuman Publishers, Inc.
23 Leonard Street
New York, NY 10013

Copyright © 1989 by Neal-Schuman Publishers, Inc.

Printed and bound in the United States of America

Library of Congress Cataloging-in-Publication Data

Choosing a bibiliographic utility : user views of current choices /
    edited by Leslie R. Morris.
        p.   cm.
    Includes bibliographical references.
    ISBN 1-55570-048-9
    1. Machine-readable bibliographic data--Evaluation.   2. Library
information networks--Evaluation.   3. Bibliography--Data bases-
-Evaluation.   4. Bibliographical services--Evaluation.
5. Libraries--Automation.   I. Morris, Leslie R.
Z699.35.M28C48 1990
025.3'16--dc20
                                                            89-13582
                                                              CIP

Contents

List of Vendors

Company: AFLI
Address: Duquesne University Library, Locust Street, Pittsburgh, PA 15282
Phone number: 412/434-6136
Product: OCLC Database Services
Contact Person: Dr. Paul Pugliese

Company: Autographics, Inc.
Address: 3201 Temple Ave., Pomona, CA 91768
Phone number: 714/595-7204; 800/325-7961
Product: AGILE II Bibliographic Utility
Contact Person: George Steinbach

BiblioFile: SEE: The Library Corporation

Company: Blackwell North America, Inc. (BNA)
Address: 6024 S. W. Jean Rd., Building G, Lake Oswego, OR
Phone number: 503/684-1140; 800/547-6426
Product: B/NA Authority Control and Database Management
Contact Person: Dan Miller, Manager, Sales and Service, Technical Service Division

Company: Brodart Co.
Address: 500 Arch St., Williamsport, PA 17705
Phone number: 717/326-2461; 800/233-8467
Product: Le Pac Bibliographic Utility
Contact Person: Carol A. Rickert, Eastern Regional Sales Manager, Library Automation Division

Company: CLASS
Address: 1415 Koll Circle, San Jose, CA 95112-4698
Phone number: 408/289-1756
Product: RLIN Bibliographic Utility
Contact Person: Sharon Vaugh Shirasawa

Company: The Computer Corporation
Address: 1903 Westmoreland St., P.O. Box 6987, Richmond, VA 23230

Phone number: 800/446-2612
Product: Bibliographic Utility
Contact Person: Beth Dittles

Company: General Research Corporation
Address: 5383 Hollister Ave., P.O. Box 6770, Santa Barbara, CA
93160-6770
Phone number: 805/964-7724; 800/235-6788
Product: Bibliographic Utility
Contact Person: Darcy R. Cook, Marketing, Library Systems

Le Pac: SEE: Brodart

Company: The Library Corporation
Address: P.O. Box 40035, Washington, D.C.
Phone number: 304/725-7220; 800/624-0559
Product: BiblioFile Bibliographic Utility
Contact Person: Matt Lutz, Product Manager

Company: Marcive, Inc.
Address: P.O. Box 47508, San ANtonio, TX 78265-7508
Phone number: 512/646-6161; 800/531-7678
Product: Bibliographic Utility
Contact Person: Janifer Meldrum, Director of Marketing

Company: OCLC
Address: 6565 Frantz Rd., Dublin, OH 43017-0702
Phone number: 614/764-6000; 800/848-5878
Product: Bibliographic Utility
Contact Person: Kate Nevins, Manager, Network & Library
Service Department, Marketing & User Service Division

Company: UTLAS International U.S., Inc.
Address: 8300 College Blvd., Overland Park, KS 66210
Phone number: 800/338-8527
Product: Bibliographic Utility
Contact Person: Coordinator, Public Affairs

Preface

Fifty years ago, bibliographic utilities did not exist. Each library generated its own bibliographic data extracted from the hearts, minds, brains, experience, and training of its catalogers. Only in the mid-20th century did the Library of Congress begin to act, albeit in a primitive way, as a bibliographic utility by supplying cataloging data, first through the printed *National Union Catalog*, and later with printed catalog cards and proof slips.

In the 1970s, OCLC, utilizing primarily Library of Congress data, launched the first bibliographic utility. (Has it ever occurred to you how libraries might be different if the Library of Congress had set up a nationwide computer system before OCLC? Or if the Library of Congress had decided to set up a system in competition with OCLC?) Since the late 1970's a number of bibliographic utilities that compete with or complement OCLC have emerged.

It is incumbent on every library director, head of technical services, head cataloger, head of acquisitions, head of serials, head of public services, and all other librarians with an interest in modern librarianship working in academic, public, special, health, science, law and school libraries to have a vital interest in the range of bibliographic utility options open to his/her library. Reading this book is one of the easiest ways to learn about the full range of bibliographic utilities. Library school faculty and students also need this data for their classes.

Each library must choose a bibliographic utility that is best for its operation. Since each utility has unique strengths, there is no one system, even OCLC, that is best for all libraries. Not all bibliographic utilities have an interlibrary loan module.

If interlibrary loan is important to your library, obviously a bibliographic utility without it is of little value to you. If, however, your region or state has alternative interlibrary loan access, you may be able to live without it.

All bibliographic utilities are expensive, but each has a different pricing algorithm. Bibliographic utility "A" may be more expensive than bibliographic utility "B" in library "X," but "B" may be more expensive than "A" in library "Y." How your library uses its utility will affect the total cost. Although one utility may have lower initial and installation costs, its ongoing costs may be higher. The correct way to estimate costs is to add the installation, start-up, and one-time costs to the estimated five year operating costs. You will then be able to compare total costs.

A number of years ago, as Head of Technical Services at the State University of New York, Fredonia, when SUNY/OCLC was formed, I assisted in the installation of OCLC. Later, I became the Director of the Library at Xavier University in Louisiana where I insisted on the installation of OCLC as a condition of employment. I am now at Niagara University, where we have had OCLC for many years, and our retrospective conversion is complete. Therefore, I consider myself an "old hand" at OCLC. However, as a library director, I feel that I must stay current with developments in library technology (and other areas) in order to be sure that we are utilizing the best, most efficient, and most effective systems available.

Trying to examine all of the bibliographic utilities available is difficult. The printed literature from the vendors is sometimes vague, and at ALA conferences there is never enough time to wait in long lines or take more than a cursory look at each product. That is why we decided to organize a conference so librarians could go to one place to see all of the bibliographic utilities and choose the one best suited to their needs. It gave them a chance to examine virtually all the systems offered and learn from the experiences of those who had used each system.

The conference was called "Choosing a Bibliographic Utility: A Users' View of Current Choices" instead of "Choosing a Bibliographic Utility: Alternatives to OCLC" because that was not our theme. OCLC was well represented.

If you work in a library that uses OCLC and decide, after looking carefully at all the other possibilities, that OCLC is best for your library, you have done your duty. The object is not to change for change's sake, but only to know that you have studied all of the options and chosen the best one for your library. On the other hand, there are some very well-designed systems on the market, which are described in the text by experienced librarians who have chosen them instead of OCLC.

In an effort to standardize comparisons between systems, each author covers a number of topics including:

- size of the database
- quality of the database
- sources of the database

- ease of use
- name authority control
- subject authority control
- interlibrary loan
- acquisitions
- serials
- support to an online public access catalog
- offline products: serials lists; new acquisitions lists; COM catalogs; catalog cards
- start-up costs
- continuing costs
- service contracts.

Les Morris

Introduction

Strictly speaking, a bibliographic utility could be defined as a source of machine-readable cataloging records. All organizations providing machine-readable records offer other useful and attractive services as well. The bibliographic utility choice is not made in isolation; there are other relationships to be planned for and considered. References will be made throughout to such relationships; however, the trade-offs in choosing one source of bibliographic records with its attendant services over another with slightly different services will not be specifically addressed.

Choosing a bibliographic utility today is an opportunity for a win-win outcome. Librarians can provide better access to their collections—possibly to materials not in their collections—and at the same time improve the internal processing of their own materials. The environment in which the bibliographic utility choice will be made includes: a healthy and maturing library automation marketplace with a variety of choices and a more informed consumer group, librarians. While the marketplace has been maturing, librarians as a group have learned more about technology and its application to libraries. We are not in a situation where there is only one right answer, but rather in a situation where there is more than one good answer. Each local library will be able to look at its needs and make an appropriate local decision.

Let us examine needs assessment in libraries. Each library has slightly different priorities when selecting an automated service or system, depending on the users the library serves, the special needs those users have, and the way the library collects and sets policies to meet those user needs. For instance, a special library serving a firm engaged in research may placed more emphasis on a serials check-in and routing system than on a circulation system. Public or academic libraries with branches may desperately need mechanisms to identify the location and availability of particular items. In this case a circulation system would be the pressing need driving the choice of an automated service or system. The library may be looking for a single record system which relates all processing associated with a bibliographic unit to a single record. If so, the librarian is looking for an integrated system, one that normally would include an online public access catalog, a circulation system, a bibliographic maintenance system, an acquisitions system, and a serials system. Whatever the driving force for selecting automation as a solution, it will be necessary to choose a source for machine-readable bibliographic records.

In selecting a bibliographic utility, one needs to identify the priority and variety of uses for the machine-readable records, what do you intend to do with these records once you have them? That brings up some obvious questions that need to be answered. Does the library collect in all formats? Books, serials, AV, data files, sound recordings? If so, the bibliographic utility should provide records in all formats. Do you need all of your holdings information attached to the bibliographic record? For instance, if you have multiple copies of Michener's *Texas* or Samuelson's *Economics*, do you need item specific information attached to the bibliographic description? Is it enough to show that you have *Newsweek* with a beginning date only, despite the fact that some volumes are in microform and some are in hard copy? Does it make sense in your situation to maintain a serials list with specific holdings information? If so, how will that be accomplished? If you intend to move bibliographic data from a cataloging system to a circulation system, the item-specific information becomes important both in terms of multiple copies of monographs and bound volumes of serials. In that case, the relationship of the bibliographic data to the inventory control data must be carefully defined and linkages provided.

Regardless of the choice of bibliographic utility, the questions continue. How will you maintain the data locally? How will you correct mistakes in cataloging? Withdraw a copy? Will you change that locally in real time, or will some other mechanism for updating be available? That brings up the question of timeliness. What do you need in terms of timeliness? It's easy to say immediate. Can your library afford that? There are ways to provide access without all additions, changes, and deletions being reflected in your local automated tools immediately. While this is not a suggestion that it is appropriate for catalogs to be three months out of date, it is a decision that needs to be made considering all library needs and the cost of meeting these needs.

Now on to a soapbox issue; let us call this the bibliographic obligation. Libraries have made great strides in sharing resources through shared use of large bibliographic utilities. These utilities have become de facto *National Union Catalogs*. As more sources of bibliographic records become available, the possibility exists that the largest utilities will no longer represent the wealth of our libraries. As local choices are made for the purchase of machine-readable bibliographic records, consideration should be given to the mechanism which will provide access to users outside the library's primary user group. Tape loading to one of the utilities is a possibility as is coordinated telecommunication linkage which does not require users to dial all of our local systems directly. While there is significant overlap of collections among libraries of similar sizes and types which serve similar users, each library has unique resources. This refers to what we have come to call rare materials as well as local history. In our urgency to select an appropriate source for bibliographic records, let us not forget that no library can serve all of its users needs and that we are dependent on the holdings of all libraries.

Once you have identified your needs, it is imperative that you inventory available resources. Resources include not only money but library staff and data processing expertise. As you look at sources of bibliographic records and think about how you would utilize them in your local situation, be aware of the resources that will be required both on a one-time basis and on a continuing basis. These resources have costs, and our budget authorities don't like surprises any more than managers do.

In the area of staff expertise, consider whether current staff is prepared to write specifications for selecting a bibliographic utility, to select the utility, to negotiate a contract, to implement the service, and to provide training both to the current and future staff, and to integrate the bibliographic utility with other automated systems which you have or intend to have. For one-time needs it may be appropriate to hire a consultant. Keep in mind when working with a consultant that you are choosing a bibliographic utility for your use and stay involved in the process. The consultant will leave, but the responsibility for the decision stays. The vendor will be able to provide assistance in training, but local utilization is the responsibility of each library.

An absolute in the choice of a bibliographic utility is adherence to MARC standards. The reason to insist on the MARC standard is transportability. The choice that you make today may be the optimal choice, but in five to seven years there will be better choices and the library needs to be in a position to move data from one system to another without expensive and time-consuming processing to get non-standard bibliographic data back into the MARC format. Make sure that you own your data so that when you are ready to transport it, it belongs to you. If you already have machine-readable data from another source, you must be able to describe this data to a vendor so the vendor can work with the records.

If you will require local data processing support, negotiate the basis upon which it will be supplied for the protection of the library. Build rapport with the data processing staff and learn their jargon as you teach them library jargon. Data processors are professionals and many become intrigued by the requirements of libraries. Local data processing support may not be required depending on how you decide to meet your own needs. While the choice you make may not require software support, whatever choice you make will require hardware support. Plan for maintenance support of your hardware.

Once you install a local system, you must be prepared to pay for it not just the first time, but in the future as well. Therefore, as you look at services, consider the continuing costs. You may not buy card cabinets, but you will buy equipment, provide maintenance, and continue whatever service you select.

It is our job as librarians to be able to articulate our needs. We all have great expectations of what automation can do for our users and our ability to provide efficient service to them. Make sure that at the same time you are articulating your needs, that you hear and understand what is available in the marketplace. In the best of all possible worlds the needs assessment plus the available resources will equal an appropriate choice for a bibliographic utility. This equation can become unbalanced easily if the expectations described in the needs assessment are unrealistic.

Sherrie Schmidt

1

The Computer Corporation

John W. Zwick

Growing up in Oklahoma in the late 1940s, I entertained the usual boy's Western fantasies about cowboys and horses, good guys and bad guys.

I'll never forget going to my first rodeo. Seeing a grown man violently thrown from a wildly twisting, bucking horse quickly brought me down to earth too. That animal in no way corresponded to my fantasy of horses as noble, placid vehicles.

Then the rodeo announcer called out, "Hey kids! Look over at the green gate for something special we have for you future broncobusters. Little Jimmy Williams, who's nine years old is going to ride a romping, stomping, mean-devil pony. Here he comes out of the gate, now!"

Well, Jimmy Williams just managed to stay on that pony until they rang the bell. The fact that I was also nine helped me realize that most boys aren't ready to jump on a full-size bronco.

Just as little boys shouldn't ride broncos that are too big and mean for them, Tidewater Community College's professional staff was too small and lacked the background to work with sophisticated online cataloging utilities. Nevertheless, it was clear to us that we needed the kind of centralized cataloging and processing that such utilities can provide.

Our system is served by three libraries separated geographically. For years, if each library bought a title, we were condemned to catalog it three times. Worse, we had no union catalog of the three campus libraries' holdings. The only way students and faculty could find out what the other libraries held was by phone—a slow, error-prone procedure.

After reviewing the features of several utilities, we decided to start slowly with an offline batch processing retrospective conversion service offered by The Computer Corporation (TCC) of Richmond. They started us off with custom-designed software on floppy disks which ran on Apple computers.

One library already owned an Apple, one was able to borrow one, and the Virginia Beach Campus library staff drove to the Chesapeake Campus library and used theirs a few hours each week.

This offline procedure amounted to nothing more than our cataloging clerk keying in LC card or ISBN numbers, abbreviated author and title entries, and then comparing call numbers for hits on TCC's database on the floppy disk.

Hits were recorded on a formatted data disk in the second drive. Each library then mailed its disks (identified with its initials) to TCC which compiled a union catalog on computer tape with location designations for each campus.

This interim service provided us with a computer output microfiche (COM) catalog of the holdings of the three libraries, which was updated every six months for the first year of the retrospective conversion project. The libraries also received editing reports in the form of weekly fiche and paper printouts containing records of the most recent input relative to: multiple hits; possible hits; and no hits.

In the spring of 1986, TCC delivered an offline software system in IBM-PC/MS-DOS format. The Virginia Beach and Frederick Campuses adopted this version for the balance of 1986 while the Chesapeake Campus continued to use Apple.

By January 1987, the administration provided IBM compatible terminals for each library, and we contracted with TCC for online service. Now, each of the three libraries could input records and receive immediate confirmation of a valid hit. We were getting there.

The next step was to reach out to Virginia's 23 other community colleges. Methodologies for retrospective catalog conversion were discussed during an annual conference of the Virginia Community College Association. Our data processing manager then wrote to everyone asking if any of them were interested in utilizing the Virginia Community College System's regional computer telecommunications network to carry online searching for retrospective catalog conversion with TCC. This would eliminate all long distance line charges for terminal hookups since the five community college regional computer networks were each tied into the Virginia Community College System's IBM mainframe in Richmond. Queries from the remote college terminals could be relayed via computer telecommunications directly to TCC's IBM mainframe computer.

More than half of the 23 colleges signed on. The direct line between TCC and VCCS computers was installed and is now operational.

Since Tidewater Community College's libraries graduated to online terminal use, monthly input rate has quadrupled.

The Computer Company's *Release Five* is now installed and serving all online customers. Along with existing searching, claiming, and original cataloging functions, new service features planned are:

1. Full-screen editing capabilities to reconcile a library's exact holding with TCC's database.
2. Software enhancements allowing a remote user to make on-screen edits and have them saved, encouraging the user to take a more active role in making real-time edits.

A desirable future utility would be programming to enable the electronic capture of a record by the remote user at his or her terminal or, in other words, real-time, current cataloging. This would allow us to move the record for a new title into the Virginia Tech Library System (VTLS) online catalog, for example.

Tidewater Community College is currently on schedule to complete retrospective conversion and obtain our holdings tapes to load with the VTLS online catalog. The College owns a Hewlett-Packard 3000 minicomputer with 43 terminals which will be updated and upgraded to support VTLS's online catalog, circulation, and serials modules.

The staffs of our three libraries have grown in their abilities to work with TCC's sophisticated online cataloging utility, even though we started on something slower and simpler. We're planning to continue with it because they've enhanced their services and have grown right along with us.

My nickname for the Virginia Tech Library System On-Line Catalog and Circulation Utilities is "Thunderbolt." I'm confident that in another year we'll be ready to ride Thunderbolt.

2

Research Libraries Information Network

Phoebe Ruiz-Valera

The Library of the Association of the Bar of the City of New York is one of the oldest and largest private law libraries in the country. It was founded in 1871 to serve the needs of both researchers and practitioners. It has over 500,000 volumes and is a member of the local network with Columbia University and New York University.

The Research Libraries Information Network (RLIN) was selected as the bibliographic utility because all three members of the local network are members of it and use it for cataloging and interlibrary loan. Each library can customize its own records according to local practice and still take advantage of contributed cataloging. It also permits each library to pass records to a local automated system.

RLIN is an integrated, automated information network owned and operated by its members through a nonprofit organization called Research Libraries Group, Inc. (RLG). The members of RLG are mostly large university libraries much as Columbia, Stanford, Harvard, etc., but it also offers associate membership and services to special and smaller libraries. It brokers its services through CLASS. The different membership categories deal with the governance and administration of the network and do not affect the services that libraries receive from RLIN. These services consist of shared cataloging, acquisitions, interlibrary loan, collection development, and support for bibliographical and reference services.

The Association of the Bar of the City of New York has been using RLIN since 1980. We use the technical processing subsystem for cataloging and producing cards and tapes. Since there are many university law libraries on RLIN, we find about 80 percent of our materials cataloged already and we can add our local subject headings and classification. This allows the catalogers more time to concentrate on original materials and problems. One advantage of RLIN is that it allows us to compare the cataloging done by different libraries for difficult items and select the treatment we prefer.

We use RLIN for acquisitions. Some applications are: pre-order searching since it shows your own library's record first if it is in a catalog cluster; determination of whether to process an invoice when the publisher, title, or author is not clear. (Through keyword search we can determine if we have received the item.) Also, RLIN helps us answer questions on ordering information since most LC records contain the price and the MARC field for the publisher's address. Further, we use it to determine the catalog entry for adding our supplements and pocket-parts, which may have a different compiler each time. Our reference department uses RLIN constantly to compile subject bibliographies, for interlibrary loan information, and to assist patrons who cannot use the paper catalog because they do not have an exact title. It helps our binding clerk locate libraries that have the same material we do so we can fill in gaps in our holdings. We are counting on being able to load the RLIN tapes to bring up an online catalog on our local INNOVACQ system.

The system groups member's records into clusters for the same title and edition of a work. A search will produce a multiple display showing the records in a Primary (PRI) format with an author, title, publication data display and the library ID's of libraries cataloging that item for their collections (Tables 1 and 2). You can select specific libraries within each cluster and view their records, including local notes and particular call numbers and holdings. If your own record is part of the cluster, it will display first, in partial form (PAR) with author, title, publication information, call number, and holding notes (Tables 3 and 4). The types of displays can be changed according to your needs. For work in Technical Services there is a FULL display mode which shows all of the MARC tags and fields for the records (Tables 5 and 6). For Reference purposes there is a LONG form which displays users records in the familiar catalog card form with notes, subject headings (Tables 8 and 9).

Table 1: Primary Display (BKS File)

```
PROD     Books      PRI      NYPG794301677-B       Search          CRLG-JRB
Cluster 2 of 3
+B
Bartlett, Donald L.
  Empire : the life, legend, and madness of Howard Hughes / by Donald L.
Bartlett and James B. Steele. 1st ed. New York : Norton, c1979.
  687 p.; ill.: 24 cm.

  ISBN 0393075133
  LCCN: 791331
  L.C. CALL NO: CT275.H6678 B37 1979
  ID: NYPG794301677-B            CC: 1665      DCF:
- - - - - - - - - - - - - - - - - - - - - - - - - - - - - - - - - - - - - - -
NYPG (c-1665 NN)    AZFG (c-9610 AzF)    AZPG (c-9610 AzTPC)    CPCG (c-9610 CF)
CMCG-1 (c-9616 COMC)    CMCG-2 (c-9610 COMC)    CNBG (c-9610 CStrNB)
COSG (c-9665 CoFS)    CPAG (c-9610 CPa)    CRLG (b-9665 CStRLIN *a*)
CRPG (c-9610 CRic)    CSCG (c-9666 CSjCL)    CSFX (c-9610 CSf)
CSUG (c-9610 CSt)    CSUU (c-9610 CSt)    CTYG (c-9665 CtY)    CUBG (c-9610 CU)
CUBU (c-9610 CU-BANC)    CUDG (c-9610 CU-A)    DCLC (c-9110 DLC)
ILEG (c-9610 IE)    ILNG (c-9665 IEN)    MDJG (c-9665 MdBJ)    MIUG (c-9610 MiU)
NHDG (c-9665 NhD)    NJRG (c-9610 NjR)    NVRG (c-9110 NvU)    NYBG (c-9665 NBiSU)
NYCG (c-9110 NNC)    NYCX (c-9665 NIC)    NYUG (c-9665 NNU)    PATG (c-9665 PPT)
PAUG (b-9665 PU)    UTBG (c-9610 UPB)
```

Note: A non-Roman record displayed in PRI will have a bracketed code for the record's non-Roman script(s) to the right of the DCF field and also following the holding library's NUC code.

A microform record containing a value for GEN in the fixed fields will have the GEN values set off by asterisks following its LI/NUC string (see the CRLG record in the holdings above). A record containing no GEN but having a value for QD will have a plus ("+") in this position.

We are satisfied with the way the system operates. Sometimes it is slow or goes down, especially when they are "improving" the hardware or software; but we find that it is less time-consuming to wait for it to come back up again than to deal with the work manually. It usually comes back up within the same day and we get advance warning of any plans to bring it down for any extended periods.

RLIN issues error report forms to libraries to correct typos or problems with a record. These high technical standards mean that we can use contributed cataloging. Periodically, RLIN publishes "Operations Update," a newsletter discussing ways to improve our use of the system. One of the problems of being a CLASS library is that sometimes these mailings are delayed since RLIN sends them to CLASS to distribute. However, both RLIN and CLASS coordinators are very helpful in solving problems.

Table 2: Interpreting the PRImary Display Format

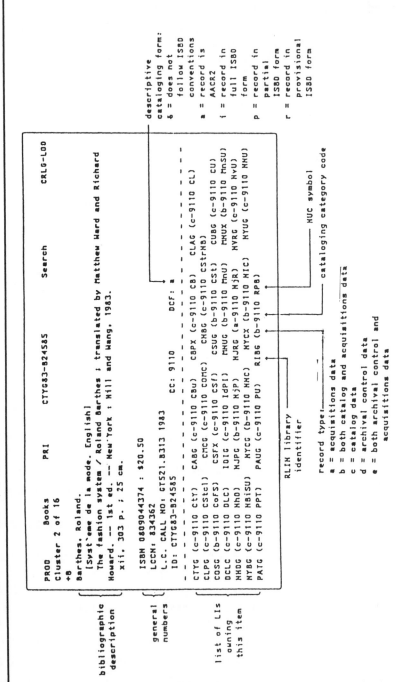

Table 3: PARtial Display (BKS File)

```
PROD     Books      PAR      CRLG83-B242           Search       CRLG-MMK
Cluster 2 of 3
+
Bartlett, Donald L.
  Empire : the life, legend, and madness of Howard Hughes  [microform] / by
Donald L. Barlett and James B. Steele. New York : Norton, c1979.
  687 p.; ill.: 24 cm.

  ISBN 0393075133
  LCCN: 791331
  L.C. CALL NO: CT275.H6678.B37 1979
  ID: CRLG83-B242               CC: 9115      DCF:
- - - - - - - - - - - - - - - - - - - - - - - - - - - - - - - - - - - -
CT275.H6678B37 1979

STK
   c.2   (LOS 12/12/84)
      Acq: 83-B242-1.

UND    CT273.H6678385 1979
   c.1   (CAT 05/06/84)
      Acq: 83-B242-1.
- - - - - - - - - - - - - - - - - - - - - - - - - - - - - - - - - - - -
 UID 83-B242-1        UTYP UO   LSI              CPST CAT 05/06/84  UST P

 UID 83-B242-2        UTYP UO   LSI              CPST ORD 02/23/86  UST P
 QTY 1   SID MXG      CURR      LPRI $25.00
SUPN BLACK
        Replacement for STK copy.
 ORD  02/23/86   STK
```

Note: A non-Roman record displayed in PAR will have a bracketed code for the
      record's non-Roman script(s) to the right of the DCF or PROC field (whichever
      is last on the line.)

      An AMC record displayed in PAR will have archival control data where the above
      record's holdings data is located (following the bibliographic data).

      See also "Interpreting the PARtial Display Format."

In order to save money, shared local networks on RLIN are possible with nearby libraries using one terminal for cataloging. Since libraries can see each other's holdings, arrangements can be made for interlibrary loans and even distributed collection development. During the summer of 1984, we used the RLIN terminals at New York Public Library, which they graciously allowed us to do while the Bar renovated the library. (Our new location wasn't available for three months.) You can use another library's terminals to produce work because your own account is billed for the CPU's used and for the products.

In conclusion, many libraries like the nationwide search capability on RLIN; smaller libraries like the idea of typing their own cards inhouse based on cataloging from LC or Harvard. Although

Table 4: Interpreting the PARtial Display Format

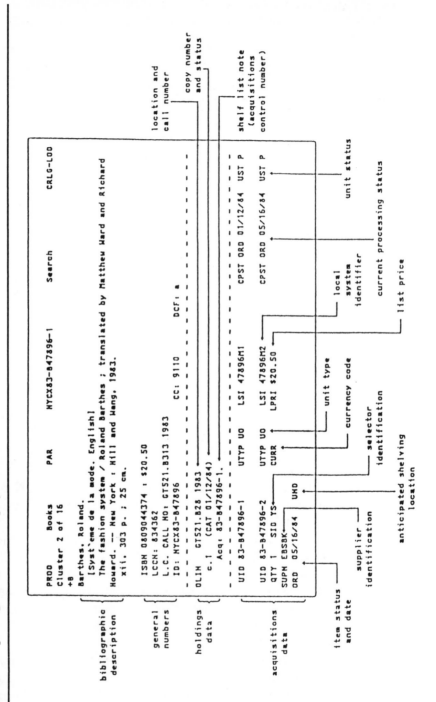

Table 5: FULly Tagged Display—BIBliographic Segment (BKS File)

```
PROD      Books       FUL/BIB   CRLG83-B242              Search              CRLG-MMK
Cluster 2 of 3
+
  ID:CRLG83-B242     RTYP:b    ST:p   FRN:    NLR:     MS:  EL:  AD:11-03-83
  CC:9115  BLT:am    DCF:      CSC:   MOD:?   SNR:     ATC:      UD:02-23-86
  CP:nyu   L:eng     INT:      GPC:   BIO:b   FIC:0    CON:
  PC:r     PD:1982/1973        REP:a  CPI:0   FSI:0    ILC:a     MEI:?   II:?
  MMD:a    OR:?  POL:u    DM:u    RR:a---  COL:c    EML:u     GEN:a  BSE:u
  010      791331
  020      0393075133
  040      ‡cNN‡dNN‡dCStRLIN
  050      CT275.H6678‡bB37 1979
  100 10   Bartlett, Donald L.
  245 10   Empire :‡bthe life, legend, and madness of Howard Hughes ‡h[microform]
           / by Donald L. Barlett and James B. Steele.
  260      New York :‡bNorton,‡cc1979.
  300      687 p.;‡bill.:‡c24 cm.
  500      Includes bibliographical references and index.
  533      Microfilm.‡bStanford, CA :‡cResearch Libraries Group,‡d[1982]‡e 1 reel
           . 35 mm.
  600 10   Hughes, Howard Robard,‡d1905-1976.
  651  0   United States‡xBiography.
  700 10   Steele, James B.,‡ejoint author.
```

Note: On a Roman-only terminal or on a non-Roman terminal with a scripts setting of
    "ROMan", you will see only Roman-alphabet fields in the FUL display; an
    abbreviation for any non-Roman script in the record will appear as the last
    element on the message line for each page of the BIB segment.

RLIN is a sophisticated, automated system aimed at large research libraries with many branches, its resources can be used by libraries of all sizes and interests and you can expand or narrow its use to your convenience and to meet the needs of your library.

Table 6: FULly Tagged Display—HOLdings Segment (BKS File)

```
PROD      Books      FUL/HOL   CRLG83-B242            Search          CRLG-MMK
Cluster 2 of 3
+
                                            CIN FRG   OID LOD   FD 11/03/83
     CALL CT275.H6678‡bB37 1979
     VOL
     ANT
     INS          EXT
     HST 12/12/84 N, 05/06/84 C
     FNT                              PTH       FSP

     LOC STK      LCAL
     LVOL
     LANT
     LINS         LEXT
     LHST 12/12/84 N, 05/06/84 C
     LFNT                             LPTH      LFSP
        COP 2            MDES
        CST       LOS 12/12/84
        CCAL
        SHNT ‡q83-B242-1
        COP             MDES
        CCAL
        SHNT
```

```
PROD      Books      FUL/HOL   CRLG83-B242            Search          CRLG-MMK
Cluster 2 of 3
+

     LOC UND      LCAL CT273.H6678385 1979
     LVOL
     LANT
     LINS         LEXT
     LHST 05/06/84 C
     LFNT                             LPTH      LFSP
        COP 1            MDES
        CST       CAT 05/06/84
        CCAL
        SHNT ‡q83-B242-1
```

Table 7: FULly Tagged Display—Acquisitions Segment (BKS File)

```
PROD      Books      FUL/UNIT  CRLG83-B242-2         Search        CRLG-MMK
Cluster 2 of 3
+
Bartlett, Donald L./Empire : the life, legend, and madness of Howard Hughes  [m
   UTYP UO      DP Y     CPST ORD 02/23/86 LOD          UID 1
   UST P                 FPST CLA 06/23/86              UAD 02/23/86 LOD
    SID MXG     LSI

   SUPN BLACK
   SHIP ACQ    MCI 4     RUSH        NCC 4      NCS 0      TAPE
   BILL        ICI 1     DAC                    LSAC
   SICO PBK
   SINT
   SCAT
    DRR
   DRRH
   CTNT Replacement for STK copy.
```

```
BKS/TEMP  Books     FUL/MAT   CRLG83-B242-2         Search        CRLG-MMK
Record 1 of 1
+
Bartlett, Donald L./Empire : the life, legend, and madness of Howard Hughes  [m
UTYP UO     MLOC STK      MPST ORD
   ISBN 0393075133
   QTY 1
   MAT
   LPRI $25.00           LPD Y           EDRT
   CURR

   FUND

   ICL                   ICAD
```

Note: Acquisitions segments can only be seen by the owning institution, although
      some acquisitions data appears on the PARtial display.

Table 8: LONg Display (BKS File)

```
PROD      Books     LON      CRLG83-B242           Search        CRLG-MMK
Cluster 2 of 3
+B
Bartlett, Donald L.
  Empire : the life, legend, and madness of Howard Hughes  [microform] / by
Donald L. Barlett and James B. Steele. New York : Norton, c1979.
  687 p.; ill.: 24 cm.

  Includes bibliographical references and index.
  Microfilm. Stanford, CA : Research Libraries Group, [1982] 1 reel.  35 mm.
  ISBN 0393075133

  1. Hughes, Howard Robard, 1905-1976. 2. United States--Biography. I. Steele,
James B., joint author. II. Title.

  LCCN: 791331
  L.C. CALL NO: CT275.H6678.B37 1979
  ID: CRLG83-B242            CC: 9115     DCF:
  CALL: CT275.H6678B37 1979
```

Note: A non-Roman record displayed in LON will have a bracketed code for the
      record's non-Roman script(s) to the right of the DCF field.

Table 9: Interpreting the LONg Display File

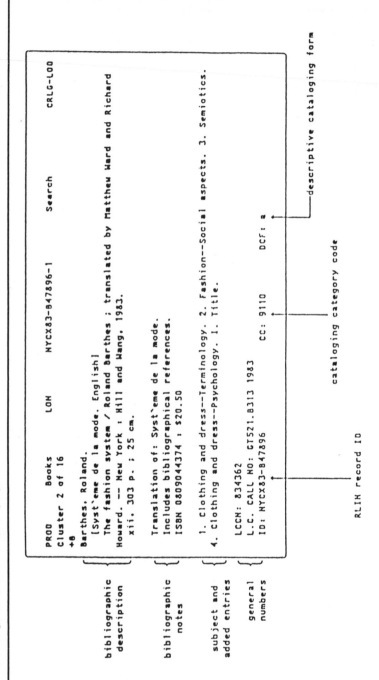

3

The Library Corporation: Bibliofile

Sally Knight

In 1984 New York State passed legislation which permanently established school library systems. One of the new regulations charged these systems with developing a database of the holdings of member school libraries in machine-readable format (Library of Congress MARC) for the purpose of interlibrary loan. These records were to be compatible with others in the state, the ultimate goal being a catalog of all New York State libraries' holdings.

Each of the 46 school library systems, minimally funded for such an automation project, was given carte blanche as to the means of developing its database. The many vendors who supply Library of Congress cataloging records offered workshops, gave talks, and sent voluminous information to directors of the systems. Out of all of the choices available, I selected The Library Corporation (TLC) for the Cattaraugus-Allegany School Library System, a choice based on cost and ease of use.

TLC has been a database publisher since 1974, specializing in bibliographic information for libraries and bookstores. It has produced COM fiche, MARCFICHE with Library of Congress cataloging, for the past 10 years, serving more than a thousand libraries.

In 1983, TLC began conducting laser storage application, design, and feasibility studies. In early 1984, they demonstrated a working prototype using a Laser Data device. By late 1984, the capability to load and to efficiently access bibliographic data stored on CD-ROM (Compact Disk-Read Only Memory) was created. Bibliofile was announced and demonstrated at the American Library Association mid-winter meeting in January 1985. Production deliveries began in February, and over 1,000 libraries around the world are now using it.

Bibliofile runs on an IBM or PC compatible with a 512K memory recommended. The initial purchase provides a CD-ROM reader, search software, database and documentation, and new cumulative editions of the database, either monthly or quarterly, depending upon which subscription you choose. The initial cost of an IBM-AT and the Bibliofile subscription has provided me with a workstation that also can be used for other computer functions and CD-ROM functions. For $870 the laser disks are updated quarterly. Monthly updates cost $1470. This is the only ongoing cost, as there are no online telecommunications charges. Bibliofile can be used at any time, without waiting for other systems or suffering down time, and searching can be prolonged as necessary because there are no online charges. To me, this is its greatest selling point, especially for those on limited budgets.

Bibliofile's database of three million MARC records gives access to all Library of Congress English records: monographs, serials, Government Printing Office publications, music, film, maps, and Canadian publications. These three million records reside on four compact laser disks and belong to you.

Cattaraugus-Allegany School Library System (CASLS) librarians send copies of their shelflist cards, marked with their school name and the ISBN (International Standard Book Number) or LCCN (Library of Congress Card Number) of the item, to the CASLS office for input into our database.

Bibliofile's *Catalog Production System* is menu driven and allows you to search the laser disk database by author, title, ISSN, ISBN, LCCN or GPO number. The search can be narrowed by publication year, type of material, or author's name.

Armed with our shelflist cards and their information and Bibliofile's searching options, this simple procedure begins: our access software has been installed on a Corvus hard drive so we turn on the computer, bring up BIB, put laser disk No. 4 (the index) in the CD-ROM reader drawer. The opening and closing of the drawer holding the laser disk is the slowest part of the operation. The menu shown on the next page appears.

It is fastest to search using the ISBN or LCCN. The database is searched and the full MARC record appears on the screen. Every indicator and subfield is shown and can be added to, deleted or changed by moving the cursor and using the editing key. Your holding location code is automatically inserted in the record and shown on the screen. CASLS also adds the local Dewey number. Once all editing is completed, the record is stored on floppy disk by striking F9. The records stored on floppy disks can be searched sequentially by using the left and right cursor keys or by scanning the contents of the entire disk. A separate floppy disk is used for each of our multiple schools.

Figure 1: Bibliofile Master Menu

```
Select an application from the menu by pressing the key listed to the
left of the function.

        CATALOG PRODUCTION:                    BOOK ACQUISITIONS:

        C = Catalog Production                 L = LaserSearch Acquisitions
        F = Foreign CPS
        S = Configure CPS
        U = Batch Utilities

        OTHER APPLICATIONS:

        E = Electronic Encyclopedia
        X = Exit to DOS
```

The software for Bibliofile now permits queuing of records. When the No. 4 index disk is searched and a record found to be resident on Laser Disk 1, 2, or 3, the record is automatically stored or queued. At the end of each input session or at the beginning of the next, in response to the question: Retrieve disk queue from output diskette (Y/N)? and answering yes, those records are brought up on the screen and matched against the appropriate laser disk for storage on a floppy, a great time-saving device.

Floppies can be converted to OCLC-type magnetic tapes, or to any format specified, for archiving or for downloading to local circulation, catalog or other systems. The Catalog Production System has been interfaced to library computer systems supplied by other vendors, making it possible to transfer MARC data directly from your microcomputer to several systems such as a circulation or an online catalog.

Using the Configuration System allows you to customize your records, as we do by adding the local holding code. This also allows you to do original cataloging by providing custom tailored fields. It is also possible to see records in catalog card format and to print catalog cards and labels.

CD-ROM readers can be stacked and four laser disks can be searched at a time. CASLS has two laser readers connected to the computer; searching two disks at a time speeds up the procedure considerably. Multiple printers can also be used.

TLC also offers other features, such as run in *Enhanced Bibliofile*, which has options to upgrade catalog production to an independent catalog maintenance or processing center system, custom designed for each library's requirements. It is possible to add up to eight workstations, connected to a basic system and sharing a local MARC database. It is also possible to add a barcode reader to augment MARC records with circulation information.

TLC's *Any Book* is a book identification and ordering database which is updated, recompiled, and replaced quarterly. One laser disk gives access to almost every book published in the English language during the past 15 years, plus earlier titles known to be recently out of print.

The system automatically displays all pertinent information on an order form, calculates prices, and checks whether the book is already on order. With a modem, the order can be sent electronically or it can be printed on standard forms. The system checks in orders received, noting what remains on order, and checks the status of all accounts, orders, and titles.

Bibliofile Intelligent Catalog is a stand-alone, CD-ROM-based public-access catalog. It offers three powerful searching approaches, each activated by a labeled function key or a choice from the main menu: Find Anything, View Catalog, Browse Topics. It has an audio help system with advice and suggestions, triggered after a period of inactivity or in response to the HELP or TUTOR keys. The hardware is a CD-ROM reader and a hard disk to which supplemental files of bibliographic information, more recent than that on the current laser disk, are stored. New files are transferred using magnetic media and copied on the hard disk. This *Intelligent Catalog* is a low cost answer to providing a stand alone public access catalog.

At CASLS, we started entering records of new nonfiction purchases for elementary and secondary schools and the hit rate has run between 75% and 90%. This year, in addition to new purchases, we entered all of the Dewey Class 800 (Literature). There were many very old books, and the hit rate has been 73 per cent. Although Bibliofile provides for original cataloging of the items not found, CASLS sends these records to another vendor to be included in the production of their fiche catalog. The minimal cost for this service is less than the cost of doing original cataloging.

TLC, while the best choice for CASLS, does have some drawbacks. Perhaps the most serious are: items not included in the Library of Congress database; audiovisuals that schools purchase; rebound books; and older materials or materials from small presses. The manual is also a negative, proving to be very confusing not only to the novice but even to the computer literate.

Four school library systems in Western New York are now using Bibliofile to produce their database. In time, when the number of records is large enough, a joint catalog could be produced on laser disk. To date, CASLS has produced a microfiche catalog, updated this year, from the records created by Bibliofile on floppy disks. Fifty-three libraries have copies of the fiche catalog. This would not have been possible in an online system with its high telecommunications costs. CASLS was able to set up an interlibrary loan network immediately at minimal cost using Bibliofile.

4

Utlas

Maurice J. Freedman
Beverly Harris

The Westchester Library System (WLS) is a cooperative public library system located in Elmsford, New York. WLS is chartered to serve the 38 public libraries of Westchester County. It provides a variety of services to the county's public libraries and primary among them is technical services.

Approximately 80 percent of all of the new books going into these libraries are bought, cataloged, and processed by WLS. The current level of production includes cataloging 20,000 new titles and processing 120,000 volumes annually. The materials handled by WLS are restricted to books. Maintenance transactions in 1986 numbered 36,000 or 26 percent of a database of 130,000 titles.

WLS became an OCLC member in 1975 but did not do all of its cataloging on OCLC until 1980, when it began to distribute the bulk of its catalog records as microfiche rather than cards.

Before 1980 only adult nonfiction was cataloged on OCLC and the bulk of cataloging records were produced on a printing press.

WLS embraced automation somewhat tentatively because of the difficulties of assuming long-term budgetary commitments to staffing and contracting in a cooperative system, governed by consensus and depending for funding upon state and county legislators. Many Westchester librarians were convinced of the potential benefits of a centrally supported automated database. That is why the overwhelming board and member library approval of a commitment to support a computer-output-microfiche catalog was so heartening.

The need to support a coherent database that would be distributed as a whole, rather than card by card, promoted a closer look at OCLC. At first, member libraries feared OCLC would have serious limitations as a provider of the sophisticated database management services needed.

Except for periodic response time problems, OCLC functioned well as a remote printer and distributor of catalog cards. It was highly successful in reducing the need for original cataloging and as a finding tool for catalog records on a first search. It allowed WLS to speed book delivery to libraries and removed the need for LC proof slips and the drudgery of retaining and filing these for catalog copy. After OCLC took over catalog records, we abandoned a very labor intensive printing operation with notable improvements for office ergonomics.

Adopting a microfiche catalog meant that all catalog records had to be in machine-readable form so they could be processed into COM. Significant authority work needed to be done. WLS had supported "see from" and "see also" name authorities in card form for member libraries. These authority decisions needed to be transferred to machine form, so WLS could guarantee that names in the catalog would agree with books on the shelf.

We had to define the scope of the catalog so that retrospective conversion resources, which at the time were meager, could at least be applied to the most frequently accessed records. For WLS this implied converting as many of the most current titles as the System could afford.

Practically, this resulted in two years of retrospective cataloging. Both titles added as a result of purchases through the system-provided central acquisitions, and books acquired locally were included in the conversion. These locally acquired titles were reflected in card form in a union catalog. These cards became input for the conversion. The fiction and juvenile titles cataloged centrally and not previously added to the OCLC database were converted. The COM catalog was to start with imprints of 1978 and later. Because WLS had subscribed to OCLC monthly archival tape services, it was possible to capture these previously cataloged titles for the COM catalog.

WLS searched for a vendor that could process the WLS bibliographic records as they appeared on the OCLC transaction file. At the time, 1979, the format of the WLS records on the OCLC tape eliminated some vendors, whose software versions were oriented toward either a first occurrence of a bibliographic record or the last occurrence of that record on tape as the authoritative cataloging record for the institution. For WLS this "authoritative record" could not be determined by the placement of its occurrence on the tape. Member libraries may order from review sources that take in a time span of 18 months or more. When a library orders a given title, it is a random event as far as central processing is concerned. The database needed to be updated as books were shipped.

WLS definitely could not undertake re-editing of its OCLC record every time a new library had its symbol added, nor did WLS wish to limit the number of order sources for its member libraries; competing vendors were quick to suggest alternatives to overcome constraints on their automated processing of OCLC tapes.

A detailed request for proposal described WLS requirements and, after reviewing it, four vendors dropped out of the bid process. Brodart submitted the winning bid and was among the very few vendors WLS could identify who would be able to compile bibliographic holdings and update transactions in a coherent file over the anticipated production periods.

WLS had formerly used OCLC to produce sets of cards for the ordering "holding libraries." With the introduction of COM, two cards were provided each separate location. All new titles, whether ordered through System central acquisitions or individually acquired by member libraries, were cataloged on OCLC by System staff. This additional cataloging role for the System was, of course, implicit in the concept of the COM catalog that would make available the display of the collective acquisition efforts of the member libraries.

COM AS A RESOURCE FOR MEMBER LIBRARIES

The distribution of the total of current cataloging records for the System provided an additional bibliographic resource for local library staff engaged in cataloging. Titles that had been independently cataloged in multiple System libraries could now be used to establish a cataloging authority to which subsequently acquiring libraries could simply add their holdings.

Another significant benefit of the distributed catalog records was that uniform authority control could be applied centrally to individual bibliographic records. This allowed catalogers and reference staff in individual libraries to take advantage of authority displays available to System catalogers from the OCLC utility and to be able to see displayed consequences of decisions made by System catalogers.

Interlibrary loan was enhanced and facilitated because all entries in the catalog displayed local holdings and allowed local libraries to contribute to the work of identifying libraries from which the interloan might be requested. A procedure was instituted requiring member libraries to verify all requests and cite the unique number of the bibliographic item in the COM catalog.

TECHNIQUE OF COM PRODUCTION

Monthly, a transaction tape of all WLS cataloging and updates was produced by OCLC and mailed to Brodart. Brodart produced a COM fiche catalog for WLS from the OCLC tape, conquering the problem of multiple bibliographic records for the same work and overlaying and cumulating holdings as appropriate. As additional input, and especially to address authority changes or additions to the LC structure, WLS staff produced voluminous sheets of typing for reading via optical character recognition devices and processing onto tape for merger with the Brodart processed OCLC records.

The catalog was produced using Library of Congress name and subject authorities. Local authority options were introduced on a quarterly basis. WLS found it possible to respond to the needs of its libraries for catalog copy that would reflect the title page; but, admittedly, these local options in authorities were limited to the most "glaring" cases. A glaring case would be, for example, books showing title page as Harry Patterson displaying under Jack Higgins, which is what happens if LC authority control prevails over the institution's ability to respond to the demands of common sense.

Nevertheless, by retaining most Library of Congress subject headings in machine form and supplementing them with local name authorities, for the first time WLS was able to provide a catalog which served as a single-authority structure controlling entries for 38 independent libraries.

Cross reference standards were established across the system of libraries. Complete catalogs were produced each quarter with monthly supplements during the interim. The monthly supplements were not run against the authority program that maintained the cumulations. One reason for this had to do with how local authorities became part of the machine record.

SHORTCOMINGS OF OCR PROCESSING

It should be noted that Brodart now offers alternatives to the OCR updating technology it employed in the early 1980s. It was OCR technology, however, that was used to process large amounts of maintenance transactions to the COM database. The OCR technology required that this data be typed on specially provided sheets using an IBM selectric compatible OCR type font.

It was necessary to format the OCR record so that the kind of transaction could be later identified for machine processing, e.g. deletion, change, addition, scope note, etc. In addition, the MARC tag had to be identified, the number of the record identified, and the beginning and ending of the instruction given. Somewhere in the middle of all these characters, none of which actually formed English words for the enlightenment of the typist, the actual language to be added, deleted, or changed was recorded.

All local authority options reflected in the edited OCLC cards had to pass through this process for display in the catalog.

PROBLEMS OF VOLUME, RESPCNSE TIME, CATALOG DEADLINES

What made things especially difficult for WLS as an "OCLC/Brodart" client was the fact that the 38 member libraries were not constrained to order their books at any special time. Thus the Tech Services staff was constantly in the position of revisiting OCLC records for the purposes of adding holdings. If a particularly bulky order coincided both with slow response at OCLC and an approaching COM deadline, pressure mounted on the OCR operation, and, of course, on staff responsible for it. Thirty-eight agencies would examine the catalog for its disclosure of their holdings.

It was obviously necessary to have a clear deadline attached to the production of each catalog. This deadline was printed on the catalog header. A memo relating the deadline to book processing was included with each catalog distribution. Nevertheless, it was difficult for those not directly involved in the OCR process to recognize the steps in sequencing different kinds of input to an OCR process related to cumulations and an online process to OCLC for the bibliographic records themselves.

It seemed that there would exist a permanent disjunction in bibliographic control for external users of the catalog from the fact that authorities needed to be separately maintained and merged with the newest OCLC records. Users' impressions of staff responsiveness to authority questions were negatively affected by quarterly processing of authorities and further by "glitches" in the OCR technique itself.

In addition, there was the problem of handling holdings deletions and other maintenance transactions. These were reported by libraries as they moved books in and out of different collections from those displayed in the microfiche cataloged, or ordered or received gifts of books for which other libraries were already listed in the catalog, or withdrew copies from their collections. All of these transactions, previously processed manually in a central Union Catalog, and removed from library review, were now becoming part of a public record exposed to verification and scrutiny.

Indeed, the intense interest issues of the catalog excited was very beneficial to WLS and its member libraries because it provided additional motivation and appraisal for central staff in maintaining database quality.

MAINTAINING DATABASE QUALITY

The problems in a manual union catalog of maintaining bibliographic records and member library holdings information were exacerbated by OCLC's inability to re-display such information after it was filed. For purposes of making OCLC affordable to a system of libraries, WLS treated its members as branches though, in fact, each branch was an independent agency. This configuration created complex data strings in the 049 field. Holdings codes input by staff represented over 300 library collections identified in the OCLC profile process, which identified "holding libraries" through a series of non-mnemonic codes, e.g. Yonkers main library, adult circulation, VYZ$.

Over 150,000 of these codes had to be input by staff annually. The dexterity and attention required to input these codes accurately was invisible to libraries, who saw "sensible" designations, such as "Yon" displayed in the catalog. A typo in the OCLC code could change the holding library or remove the entire code from processing into COM.

RELIANCE ON OFFLINE DISPLAYS

To avoid re-editing the catalog record originally created on OCLC, sufficient cards were ordered to furnish each library branch with two cards. Additional cards were ordered for Technical Services files. Corresponding files of "card stock" and cataloging authorities had to be manually supported by System staff.

OCLC does not maintain online access to an institution's locally edited cataloging. That is, the Dewey number decision and any changes to the catalog record made by the local institution are not available for online recall, but must be examined from cards, worksheets, or from a display created from the OCLC transaction tape record. An exception, of course, is where the institution's cataloging is the unique or original cataloging record in OCLC. In any case, a corresponding card authority file had to be maintained for catalogers to consult between cumulations and for consistency with pre-1978 cataloging decisions.

If cataloging was revised or corrected to reflect new authority information, an interim file of such decisions had to be kept because the quarterly processing into microfiche was not current enough to allow staff to answer library questions or to record for other members of the department, decisions made by a member of the cataloging staff.

The volume of transactions that had to be accomplished was magnified by response time problems of OCLC. From time to time these response time problems were very severe. This was especially the case when WLS' overall bibliographic control processes were being re-evaluated.

Lastly, the COM catalog process with Brodart was a bit cumbersome, too. Because there was so much maintenance to do on the OCLC records, and the process of entering certain categories of maintenance transactions was especially difficult to manage within OCLC, maintenance work was done on the Brodart version of the WLS database via the OCR process. When response times at OCLC were very poor, the OCR option was used even more intensively to accommodate the large workload.

The OCLC and Brodart combination was workable, but awkward. It required supplementing from extensive offline files to provide the information staff and libraries needed. The complex steps through which data passed from OCLC to Brodart, through the added processing of Brodart's Cognitronics partner in the COM process, and the layers of documentation and file maintenance they exfoliated, presented corresponding complexity in managing staff assignments to respond to the number of dependent variables that needed to be considered.

Perhaps the most serious shortcoming of the OCLC/Brodart/Cognitronics catalog process was its complexity and the need for lay users to make judgments about its effectiveness in dealing with their individual holdings. A particular source of confusion was the OCLC printed dates on catalog cards created in advance and the possibly very different dates of the books' arrival in the library as a result of the numerous ordering opportunities, and therefore processing cycles, for the same title.

Although Utlas also prints the date of production on its cards, the inclusion of authority processing in each issue of the catalog, the reduction of holdings code blips both as the result of the new mnemonic codes enhancing operator efficiency, and elimination of OCR glitches, impressed libraries, and, therefore the Board, with the completeness and accuracy of the catalog. These perceptions made it much easier for further collective efforts on database management of local collections.

MILCS HOLDINGS

As a member of a regional consortium supported in part by New York LSCA funding, WLS had contributed approximately 200,000 monographs in the MILCS network based at the New York Public Library. These records were created under the conditions of an LSCA grant which had, as one of its goals, the compiling of a machine-readable database of bibliographic holdings of New York City regional libraries. The 200,000 titles represented one pass through the WLS union catalog, a main-entry file of the pre-1978 holdings of the 38 public libraries in WLS, as well as the holdings of 15 college libraries.

Since the MILCS commitment was ongoing, to some extent, records in MILCS duplicated records existing in machine form in OCLC and Brodart. There were about 750,000 union catalog records in card form, 200,000 of which were also in machine form in the MILCS database.

CONSIDERATION OF UTLAS

When WLS's bibliographic landscape was surveyed in 1982, a disparate picture was displayed. A pre-1978 card form union catalog, three databases, and a tape file, each of which having unique information pertaining to WLS's member library holdings, comprised the record of WLS's libraries' books.

It was the judgment of the WLS administration that such a distribution of the bibliographic resources—perhaps fragmentation is a better word—was a barrier to the user's need for access to the County's public library materials. Of the three major networks considered in 1983—OCLC, RLIN, and Utlas—only Utlas had the potential of meeting all of WLS's bibliographic control needs, needs that were dictated by the disparate databases and the WLS's Boards number one priority—further library automation.

For what WLS needed was a network with a sufficiently large database to keep original cataloging to a minimum; a network which was capable of producing offline products—specifically cards, labels and COM catalogs—in a timely fashion from its online database, thus assuring currency and accuracy; a network which maintained local holdings records and provided online access to them for the purposes of maintenance; and lastly, a mature authority control system which enabled the given library user to have machine-based quality control support.

The vendor would also have to load MILCS records from tape and convert them to a display format as close as possible to existing displays for the COM catalog. Utlas was able to load the tapes and create the desired formats in a timely way. Most important to the integration and elimination of duplicates from existing databases, Utlas was able to perform authority processing on these records that would allow for their being brought under authority control consistent with that offered by the COM catalog.

Utlas was the only one of these networks to offer all of these capabilities and services. In May, 1983, WLS decided to begin a six month experiment of using Utlas as its bibliographic utility. The project consisted in WLS cataloging a large part of its new materials on Utlas, as well as OCLC, a burden for the cataloging department because the operations were duplicated to the extent that time and labor permitted.

No effort was made to get all new materials into Utlas. OCLC was maintained as the database of record. We learned that Utlas was designed to better meet WLS' bibliographic needs than OCLC. Utlas' authority control system and its maintenance and display of local holdings were major improvements over the cataloging workload with OCLC. In addition, the response time for the terminal transactions was consistently better on Utlas than it was on OCLC.

A MUTUALLY ADVANTAGEOUS CONTRACT

At the conclusion of the six months, WLS decided that the Utlas network offered services superior to those of OCLC. A contract with favorable conditions was negotiated that served constructive and important purposes for both parties. WLS would be offered Utlas services at prices competitive with OCLC, and Brodart and would have its MILCS records loaded into the Utlas network database as part of the contractual arrangement.

Utlas agreed to WLS's requirement of daily card production and shipping, so there would be no degradation in speed of service to WLS member libraries. Other minor products and services were included but were not central to the overall decision to leave OCLC for Utlas.

Utlas gained by adding a large United States public library system to its customer base. Prior to WLS' joining Utlas, it only had one U.S. library customer, an academic library in Rochester, N.Y. Thus with WLS joining Utlas there was a greater credibility and base from which Utlas could more aggressively market its wares in the United States.

And it was precisely WLS's reason for joining that Utlas could use to prevail upon American libraries to become members of its network. The ability to create a local online database with the capabilities of editing and recalling local records enabled cataloging staff to respond much more deftly to local library needs. Lack of authority control, lack of local holdings display, clumsiness of maintenance, and problems of response time had been major shortcomings of the OCLC system. Running the Utlas pilot convinced WLS that these shortcomings could be overcome in using Utlas as its bibliographic utility. It should be noted that for the pilot project WLS had dial access to Utlas, but a direct line servicing four terminals was installed at the time of contract.

EXPERIENCE WITH UTLAS

As a network, Utlas has gone through a number of changes which have had an impact on the production at WLS and on WLS's overall relations with Utlas. In the balance of this chapter we will examine the various components of a relation with a network. For purposes of this analysis, the major areas to explore are:

1. Database performance and quality (hits found on the database and the quality of contributed cataloging).
2. Response time and database availability.
3. Customer relations (accessibility and availability of support and other staff to deal with problems, new services, training, documentation, etc.).
4. Ability to implement enhancements and changes in the system with a minimum of disruption.
5. Quality and timeliness of products.

At the conclusion of this discussion some comment will be made about Utlas as a retrospective conversion firm. By the end of 1987, WLS will have had over 200,000 records converted by Utlas, paid for by LSCA grants, and New York State Regional Database Development aid. Some comment will be made about Utlas's ability to do authority control work on these records, but it will be understood that the final products of that particular service will not have been used at the time of this writing.

DATABASE PERFORMANCE AND QUALITY

WLS contracted with Utlas in mid-November 1983. Through December 1984, just prior to the total conversion of Utlas hardware at the end of January 1985, response time and database uptime were outstanding. To meet WLS contract requirements Utlas wrote a label program that allowed WLS to process book cards and pockets from the database as WLS had done with OCLC. Suggestions from WLS about the need to expand the hours of availability were acted on, and Utlas introduced Saturday hours. The need for original cataloging increased by four percent. This four percent was almost entirely accounted for by language books previously found in the contributed cataloging of OCLC.

IMPLEMENTING ENHANCEMENTS AND CHANGES TO THE ONLINE SYSTEM

The move to new hardware (UTLAS CATSS II), about which WLS was informed at the time of contract, was designed to achieve total online, realtime access to both library bibliographic and authority records. Prior to the conversion, WLS stored online approximately two years of cataloging records. Other records were available online next day if a request was entered. WLS had a frequent need to maintain records cataloged earlier, and online access to its entire database could make more effective service it offered libraries. WLS, therefore, expected further benefits to follow from new hardware that would provide Utlas with the ability to increase online record storage for its customers.

The conversion, when it occurred at the end of January 1985, was extremely rough. WLS experienced significant problems in rendering timely service to libraries. It should be stated that Utlas attempted a truly enormous task whose successful execution continues to elude comparable bibliographic networks.

Utlas' aim was to offer each customer online access not only to a single MARC format bibliographic record, but also online, realtime access to the customer's authority records in MARC format. Authority records could be edited with cross references, scope notes, etc., exactly as the customer chose, creating an alternate authority record to those LC authorities which Utlas regularly loaded into its database. Bibliographic records and authority records and their indexes would be updated online in realtime.

The enhanced storage capability could be accessed by Boolean arguments that offered new possibilities for the solution of a variety of technical services questions that really could not be posed in comparable databases. Two examples may serve to illustrate the kinds of problem the enhanced database design could meet. A WLS library had books in a certain classification interfiled on the shelf and in the shelflist and wished to move them as a separate collection to the first floor in the library without having to count the books or the shelflist cards. WLS staff searched the database overnight for the holding library (MARC tag 090, subfield a, class, and subfield b, holding collection), and advised the library director that over 8,000 items were in the class.

In another instance, WLS was asked about the extent of university press publications in the database. Again, a Boolean search of the database using field 260, subfield b, publisher and c, date, was undertaken for acquisitions of the past 18 months, providing the information that WLS had added almost 4,000 university press titles in that period.

Utlas improved database availability after the original hardware conversion. The system now operates in a way that allows WLS generally to meet its performance criteria for service to WLS member libraries. Regrettably, WLS has not experienced the original astonishingly fast response times the early Utlas system achieved, although overall the second hardware configuration has yielded its major aim—online availability of all WLS machine readable records.

WLS has witnessed improvements in the label program and especially in the quality and design of the online authority system which give us confidence in Utlas's ability to grow in functionality and efficiency.

OFFPEAK SCHEDULING

To take advantage of faster response time when fewer users are on the system, WLS has scheduled staff for evenings, Saturdays, and weekdays from 6:30 or 7:00 A.M. Label production is always scheduled for the early morning hours because the volume of transactions required could not be achieved except during off-peak hours.

Long Boolean searches which require examination of large numbers of records are similarly scheduled for evenings or weekends. An Utlas feature which allows faster input of instructions and frees staff for other duties is a memory loop facility. This facility ensures that instructions are fed through the terminals as fast as possible, creating greater throughput even when response times are less than optimum.

The memory loop facility must be implemented by Utlas. WLS staff informs Utlas of the sequence of commands they wish to establish. Utlas then writes the code for the sequence of instruction and informs WLS when it is complete. WLS staff then invokes the loop, usually through identifying an RSN range (unique Utlas assigned identification number) to be processed against it.

Recently WLS used this feature to change indicator values on all juvenile subject headings. The memory loop consisted in identifying the entire database as the RSN range, specifying that within that range fixed field 007 should be examined for the presence of "j," and, if found, variable field 650 should be searched and indicator values in that tag changed from 1 to 0. The command to file the record back into the database is the last instruction of the loop.

Present response time can be judged from the fact that 145,000 titles were examined and changed as appropriate at a rate of three to three and a half hours per thousand or 11 seconds per record. This processing went on Saturday, Sunday after 6:00 p.m., and 6:00 p.m.-12:30 a.m. during the week.

CUSTOMER RELATIONS

WLS has enjoyed a relationship with the Utlas administration that has permitted frank discussion of problems on a regular basis. This relationship has proved most important in providing a necessary ballast during the significant organizational changes Utlas has undergone. WLS has found the constant commitment of Utlas' administration to achieving service objectives the best guarantor of Utlas services. The willingness of the administration to involve itself in critical processes and products has resulted in effective responses to WLS problems.

For WLS, Utlas's effectiveness has been impaired by the high turnover of staff responsible for dealing with services and products on a daily basis. There were frequent changes in the WLS sales representative, trainers, and a variety of individuals who were from time to time assigned responsibility for pieces of the service to the WLS account. In two years, the primary contact person changed five times.

As the first U.S. processing center staff to become Utlas users, WLS staff had the feeling that the pressure and demands member library staff subjected technical services to was poorly understood by Utlas staff. Staff had the sense that the consequences of late card deliveries or disruptions in the COM catalog schedule were not responded to with an appropriate sense of urgency. WLS staff, who serve 38 independent libraries, and the WLS director, who serves at the pleasure of the WLS Board of Trustees, had a number of reasons to view these consequences as compelling. The Utlas administration seemed to understand WLS's commitment to a high level of performance for servicing Westchester libraries and the very clearly expressed expectations of member libraries that WLS should be successful in meeting performance criteria.

A decided improvement in speed of product delivery and in quality control of products has been noted. The most serious problems WLS encountered with Utlas occurred in the two quarters following Utlas' hardware conversion.

A single account representative was recently appointed to coordinate communications. It is this person's responsibility to see that the appropriate Utlas departments are cued in to WLS projects. This representative responds to communications about retrospective conversion activities and about products and services that relate to WLS's book processing center requirements.

TRAINING

Utlas has provided WLS with effective trainers, and the documentation on which staff rely after training has improved significantly. Nevertheless—and perhaps because the Utlas CATSS II version is still fairly new—WLS staff has encountered situations or program bugs which the documentation fails to address. These situations are documented wherever possible, and printouts or descriptions of the problem are forwarded to Utlas.

The most significant of these problems was a bug in interface software to WLS's acquisition system. The interface functioned, but WLS has been frustrated in achieving the throughput expected, because the interface command would not function with the memory loop command allowing bibliographic records to be zapped into the acquisitions system without manual keying.

Utlas documentation does not at present suggest that the memory loop can only be initiated from Toronto and that the customer must call Utlas Customer Service to have the memory loop programmed. WLS discovered this when trying to invoke a memory loop from the WLS terminals.

TECHNICAL SUPPORT

The communications configuration for WLS differs from those generally used by Utlas customers, according to Utlas's technical staff. WLS experience then may be unusually intensive as well in that WLS operations typically go on for over 65 hours per week. For the most part technical staff seem well-informed and very helpful. However, there doesn't seem to be much depth, so that vacation and holiday schedules can delay responses.

WLS has four online terminals connected to a MICOM box through which the telephone line runs. One of the four terminals has a slightly different configuration to interface with a Qume Sprint printer using an RS232C interface and another terminal is configured to support the 3M Whisper printer which is the interface between Utlas and Innovacq, the acquisitions system WLS employs in its order unit.

Because the WLS communication configuration is unusual among Utlas customers, when the first line staff is not available, the configuration must be described anew to the responding technician. WLS has been fortunate in experiencing few problems. When they do occur, they can be time consuming because of the number of ports and devices that must be examined and tested.

QUALITY AND TIMELINESS OF PRODUCTS

Performance in the timeliness of products has been very much related to database performance. The COM catalog has been timely, but there have been certain problems related to the complex select criteria relating holdings information to actual processing of books for libraries. If there are unusual delays, a report is generally sent via electronic mail and is available to staff as they sign on to the database.

RETROSPECTIVE CONVERSION

WLS has provided Utlas with specifications for its conversion of certain bibliographic, audio, and video records. Utlas had successfully converted MARC tapes from both New York Public Library MILCS and Brodart in loading the initial WLS database. In doing so, Utlas provided translations of various WLS holdings and call numbers that were differently encoded in the two networks to uniform displays specified by WLS.

Because Utlas clients can maintain their own holdings display version online, codes may be input exactly as they are displayed in the COM catalog. A translation table from input to output code is eliminated. Terminal operators work with mnemonic codes that do not disappear from the online display once the online display is filed. Typos do not eliminate codes from display in the catalog, and this is marginally more helpful than having the entire code removed because of the translation table.

Sometime after the loading of MILCS records, Utlas created links from MILCS bibliographic records to the selected WLS hierarchy of authorities, namely, WLS local authorities, then Library of Congress. The mechanism through which this is accomplished is a database walk of customer bibliographic records and a refiling of these records into the customer database following an authority validation command. WLS then asked that Utlas perform a manual review of records that did not link to a valid WLS authority so keystroke errors could be eliminated. WLS then receives a printout of headings that did not match. WLS catalogers then examine the list of unmatched headings in a product Utlas calls CARP (CATSS Authority Record Printout).

The database walk step was essential in integrating the cataloging records created on the MILCS database with those to which local authority control had been applied in the COM catalog, WESTCAT database. Given the number of headings for which there were not machine readable LC authority records; however, libraries employing this step should be prepared for the inevitable impact on cataloging workloads.

This and the successful maintenance of the WLS local authority file, which includes free floating notes and references to Westchester hotlines and helplines, resulted in WLS' decision to use Utlas for the conversion of the above records. The converted records will have the same WLS local authorities applied to them as those currently applied to the COM catalog.

SIGNIFICANCE OF AUTHORITY PROCESSING

The authority process will allow standardization and enhancement by providing a cross-reference structure of local records, originally created without an authority verification process. This is particularly true of audio and video materials which Westchester libraries had cataloged without System support.

Library shelflist cards were sent to Toronto for conversion. Utlas staff received a detailed specification for the conversion of the different types of materials, along with the general instruction to provide authority links according to WLS standing practices, first a match against local authorities, secondly a match against LC authorities.

NON-BOOK CATALOGING

WLS examined OCLC, MILCS and Utlas as a provider of audio and video cataloging records. WLS found very disparate cataloging practices existing side by side in each of the databases, with all of the negatives that implies for retrospective conversion, especially for articulating cataloging policies in such areas as content notes and number and choice of added entries and analytics.

Nevertheless, to go forward with its automation future, WLS preferred to accept inevitable compromises in standardization of cataloging records to the untenable situation where member libraries would have to input audio and video recordings on an individual basis as the circulation system arrived in each library. From the very brief analysis WLS did it was clear that the hit rate would have been higher using OCLC, but in each database the amount of original cataloging required was going to require a contracted service anyway, being far beyond what could be locally addressed.

While the Utlas database was not different in reflecting very disparate audio and video cataloging practices, it was thought that the application of authorities would create enhanced local records by bringing a necessary cataloging standard to bear upon them.

Hit rates of around 60 percent on nonprint items were experienced by four WLS member libraries with significant AV collections. The conversion was effected in Toronto from library shelflists shipped by courier in a pre-arranged sequence to minimize possible logistical problems. Through its online connection to Utlas, WLS can monitor and comment upon the retrospective conversion process going on in Toronto. Arrangements are now being made for Utlas to input certain original AV titles from local library shelflist records.

AUTHORITY PRODUCTS OF CONVERSION

The CARP product is the most extensive authority product received by WLS to date. It is clear and verifiable through recall of converted MILCS records on the WLS terminals that authority links were made. The next authority product due is, indeed, the most critical one in WLS' ongoing effort to exert authority control over a variety of materials in its independent member libraries.

This product will be the tape of authority records which will be centrally loaded by WLS for the member library online circulation system. An example of a locally input authority record appears here as it is tagged for the circulation system and the current WESTCAT COM catalog. A particular concern of WLS in emphasizing authority control has been its experience in identifying multiple main entries for a single title and the consequences of this for serving member library ILL requests.

BARCODE PRODUCTION

Utlas uses the 090 field for the coding of holdings data. OCLC records coded in 049 were translated to the 090 field when these records were first loaded into the Utlas database. Thus, in the coding of holdings data, separate MILCS tape records and the OCLC/Brodart Marc tape records were made to look like current holdings records input to Utlas via online terminals, insofar as this was possible.

What complicates a smooth translation somewhat is the differently based view of call numbers in MILCS and WESTCAT. In MILCS certain collection codes appear as call number prefixes, for example, R, J, YA; whereas, in WESTCAT, they have always appeared as suffixes to library mnemonic codes displayed in the catalog.

Therefore, the specification of 090 $a, where class number appears, and 090 $b, where holdings codes appear, is quite different for MILCS and WESTCAT records. The database of origin of the cataloging records is encoded in the records themselves in two fields, 1083 and 035. They are also identifiable by the range of the RSN (Utlas record sequence number) in which they fall.

CONVERSION FROM UTLAS MARC TO US MARC

For circulation purposes, the Utlas tape outputs must again be converted for loading into the circulation database. For Utlas, this necessitates a conversion from Canadian (Utlas LHF4) MARC to US MARC where the circulation vendor's software is specified in US Marc.

This conversion is quite straightforward in terms of machine processing, but it may require thoughtful attention to rather picky details that could occupy a member of the cataloging staff for several days, depending on the variability of the originally input cataloging records and the version of MARC used by the circulation vendor. This translation process and review of the database vendor's MARC version as compared to the circulation vendor's version is necessary, of course, no matter what vendor supplies the institution's database services.

Coincidentally, Utlas's purchase of a circulation system has provided WLS with a further opportunity to integrate all aspects of its database management services to libraries. The Utlas T50 circulation system was selected by a committee representing member libraries and, upon recommendation of the WLS director, was selected by the WLS Board of Trustees.

SUMMARY

Westchester's choice of Utlas as its database vendor reflected its desire to solve particular problems related to the integration of existing databases with a need to process current cataloging most efficiently. An onerous data entry job became much more manageable by using online mnemonic codes. At the same time, this improvement in work design offered dramatically improved services to libraries through the availability of a display of locations online in real time.

The choice of Utlas also later proved most expedient upon Westchester's successful application of grant funds to address retrospective cataloging. Utlas was in a position to respond to a constraining grant schedule while effectively dealing with a wide variety of library cataloging styles that had been contributed over time to the manual Union Catalog.

5

Brodart's Online Interactive System and Lepac

Richard Panz

Within just a few years, vendors offering automated bibliographic services have proliferated from just one or two to dozens, even hundreds. This is terrific news for consumers, although it presents decision makers in library administration with an embarrassment of riches. For the Finger Lakes Library System we chose the Brodart online/interactive system which allows customers to view and manipulate their own bibliographic records (housed on a host computer in San Diego and accessed locally via Telex terminals), and the Brodart LePac or Public Access catalog on laser disk.

The Finger Lakes Library System is a state-funded cooperative serving 29 public libraries in five rural Central New York Counties. We have a total budget of $1.25 million and 35 staff members, including seven professional librarians. Our services to our member libraries include: weekly delivery of materials, consulting, graphic design and duplicating, shared AV resources, interlibrary loan and centralized ordering, cataloging, and processing of books. We also have an outreach program for agencies such as nursing homes, a books-by-mail service for shut-ins, talking book service for visually handicapped patrons, and bookmobile service.

Our technical services department processes about 30,000 books a year. These may be new books that we order or that member libraries send to us for processing. The books we turn out are shelf-ready, including catalog cards, labels, circulation cards and pockets, and book jackets. Since our formation in 1958, we have maintained a main entry union card catalog of the holdings of our member libraries to assist our interlibrary loan effort and to provide main entry authority. In 1979 we embarked on a retrospective conversion project on OCLC with the ultimate goal of converting all of our member library holdings to machine-readable form and creating a fiche union catalog that could be accessed by author, title, and subject at each of our member libraries.

Before 1976, all books were cataloged manually, catalog cards and labels were typed. In 1976, we began using OCLC to catalog our materials and produce cards. At the time, it was a much more efficient, labor saving way to catalog books. Nonetheless, we began to see ways to improve the system to better meet our specific needs. At the top of our wish list was a local bibliographic record of our own.

Our processing department sometimes catalogs 30 copies or more of a specific title. While a good number are ordered and cataloged at the same time, others arrive sporadically. Many hours of staff time have been wasted editing and re-editing the same record over and over. Since only a generic record shows on OCLC, we were constantly referring back to the hard copy union catalog for the correct form of main entry for each title. We needed to gain more quality control over items being cataloged on the system.

Our retrospective conversion project on OCLC in 1979 created a need to see the records that were being input after the workers pressed the update key. This project, which was a cooperative effort with two other library systems, converted in excess of one million records over a three-year period and was carried out by temporary staff and CETA workers. Working evenings and weekends, they were able to convert 40-60 items per hour. We saved files to spot check a large number of records, but due to the great volume, it was impossible to check even 20 percent of them.

We also needed to be able to view a four letter holding symbol on OCLC. In New York State, access for most public libraries is primarily through public library systems. Any books we catalog are displayed with our system's three-letter holding symbol, VYG. We cannot tell from the online record which of our libraries owns a particular title; we just know it's somewhere in the system. This problem grew worse as more and more of our libraries were retrospectively converted to machine readable form. Until recently, we had no complete retrospective offline product to tell us where the book was located, so we had to refuse many ILL requests from OCLC borrowers.

We began seeking a vendor/utility that could meet these needs and give us improved access to the database, with minimal staff retraining at a price within our budget. We looked at several, including Autographics, Brodart, MiniMarc, and UTLAS. Brodart met all the requirements mentioned above and impressed us with their technical staff and their willingness to listen to our wishes. Still, a decision to stray from OCLC was a major step indeed, and most likely we would not be where we are now were it not for an LSCA grant we received in 1986. Our grant has several components:

- Brodart was asked to merge all of our archival OCLC tapes and a MARC output tape of the holdings from one of our member library's automated circulation system and to create one single database of Finger Lakes System holdings.
- We were to have online access to the merged database during the grant period to add and delete records and otherwise "clean-up" the records.
- We were to test the Brodart interactive online system as an ILL and cataloging tool and compare it to OCLC.
- Finally, we hoped to create an Offline COM catalog of our database and place it in each of our member libraries.

At the end of the grant period (September 30, 1986) we judged the Brodart online system to be a superior cataloging tool and decided to continue using it with our own funds. To quote from our final grant report: FLLS tested the Brodart online system as a cataloging tool during the period July 15 through September 15, 1986. The Brodart system was deemed superior to OCLC in the following categories: ability to view local data record; efficiency of editing records; searching capability (access by author/title/keyword/subject/ISBN/LC number); ability to display member library holdings; ease of editing and creating new records on the system; ease of training staff to use system.

The Brodart system was deemed equal to OCLC in the following categories: response time, number of hours online system is available, quality of hardware. The Brodart system was deemed inferior to OCLC in the following categories: completeness of available databases; cataloging quality of some available databases; quality of catalog card production. Based on these findings and analysis of costs, the Finger Lakes Library System made a decision to continue to utilize the Brodart online system for its cataloging needs beyond the grant period.

HOW IT WORKS

Access to the system is via two Telex terminals, each with a printer. The log-on procedure is quite simple. The search screen allows us to type in the author, title, subject, keyword, ISBN, LC number, or the Brodart Access number (BAN). Hits are displayed on a summary screen that further allows the user to browse through a list of possible bibliographic choices. Once the choice is refined and selected, the computer searches a predetermined sequence of databases to find a match. In our case, our own database is searched first. If no match is found, the following are searched in order: MARC Current File; MARC Retro file; Brodart MARC; Brodart Retro; nine other public libraries from around the country; and finally Brodart GPO.

If the record is found in our own database, it is displayed in MARC format on the screen. The record displays exactly as we edited, including any changes we may have made. At this point we can modify any field, including adding or deleting the holding symbol of a library, and update the record. This stores the record, which can be recalled any time in the future. If the record is not found in our own database, the computer automatically searches the databases listed above until it locates a match. The record is then displayed on our screen and can be edited. Updated, it becomes a permanent part of our database and can be recalled at any time.

If a search does not turn up a bibliographic record from any of the databases, a cataloging screen can be displayed and an original record created. This is a fairly simple process. In fact, it is much easier than OCLC since the only standards you have to adhere to are your own. One word of caution though: a drawback to records created according to local standards is that the quality of cataloging found in other databases may not be up to your standards. Once a record is updated on the Brodart system, you can format the printing of spine, pocket, and card labels and can indicate that you want card sets to be printed. The catalog cards are printed weekly at Brodart and shipped to us in perforated sheets.

GOOD POINTS AND PROBLEMS

Some of the good points of the Brodart system include:

- full-screen editing capability, rather than line-by-line editing
- listing of individual library holding symbols by any chosen abbreviation instead of code
- ability to view your own records
- ease of creating records for items not in database
- ease of deleting bibliographic records and specific holdings from database
- Many access points to database (author, title, subject, keyword, metc.)
- ease of learning to use system (even the director can use it)
- ability to run subject and name authority for your own database.
- vendor support and willingness to tailor certain services to specific needs.

Some of the problems we have found include:

- lack of vendor-supplied, printed price schedule
- lack of support to resolve problems with equipment purchased from third party vendor
- inability of vendor to develop procedure for electronic transfer of bibliographic records to DataPhase circulation system
- numerous vendor billing errors
- less attractive than OCLC as ILL resource

Poor quality catalog cards used to be a problem. Recently, however, Brodart began using a laser printer to print cards and has seen 100 percent improvement in quality.

COSTS

Brodart has claimed that its interactive system is less expensive than OCLC since it is based on per-record storage costs and not transaction charges. We have not found this to be the case. Our experience is that the two are about equal for us. Our monthly Brodart charges include: per second storage costs (270,000 titles

@ .005/title)=$1,350; telecommunications cost $600; port access charge ($150/terminal)=$300; terminal rental ($150/terminal)=$300; printer rental ($110 each)=$220; total monthly cost=$2,470. Total yearly cost=$29,640. Our yearly OCLC costs were budgeted at $34,000, including use of the ILL subsystem. It must be noted that Brodart's catalog cards are less expensive that OCLC, $.03 rather than $.05. In an effort to hold down monthly costs, we have bought our own Telex equipment. Installation caused some problems, but our three terminals and two printers are now functioning well and we expect to see lower ongoing costs.

SUMMARY OF BRODART ONLINE SYSTEM

For us, the good points of Brodart is online system far outweigh its few problems. In most cases, Brodart has indicated that it is attempting to solve these problems. While prices are comparable to OCLC's, we feel that we are receiving a superior product much more suited to our specific needs. In addition, we feel that the Brodart interactive online system is saving us staff time, particularly as we are able to see and work with our own bibliographic records. As one of our long-term staff members put it, "I feel that our move to the Brodart system for cataloging represents and even greater leap in efficiency than our move from manual processing to OCLC. Please don't consider switching back to OCLC."

One last thing to consider: changing bibliographic utilities is not easy. As a director, I would like to have our system latch onto the newest and best bibliographic system on the marketplace. What my technical services staff keeps reminding me is that real-life implementation is much harder that just making a decision. Staff retraining and morale is a factor to ponder before making any change. Unless you are a one person library, processing a small number of books, keep in mind that others are going to have to change sometimes long-standing procedures and deal with the myriad problems that can never be predicted when you change vendors. Your staff will have to be patient and supportive. It can easily take six months or more before things start settling down into a routine.

LEPAC

Once the online system was in place and running smoothly, we were ready to cope with the last phase of our plan—creating an offline COM catalog of our database for each of our member libraries. About 90 percent of member libraries' shelflist records had been converted to machine readable form by Brodart.

We had seen demonstrations of Brodart's laser disk catalog— LePac (public access laser disk catalog)—but at first did not consider it a solution to our needs. The equipment was much more expensive than fiche readers, and we assumed that creating a laser disk containing our database would be more expensive than fiche. We were wrong. It cost slightly less. Also, it made us eligible for regional automation funds that could help pay for the laser disk equipment. With funding lined up, it was no contest. Since we were able to combine our order for 30 LePacs with another library system's order, our purchase price dropped to $2,200 each, with a full keyboard.

LePac consists of a modified microcomputer with one floppy disk drive containing software to run the system; a built-in 5.25-inch laser disk player; a laser disk containing the bibliographic records of the library; a monitor; and a keyboard that allows either short- (10-key) or full-keyboard access to the database. The 10-key model permits selecting access points and scrolling through the author/title/subject indexes. The full keyboard allows either short access mentioned above or expert searching. This latter mode allows one to type in an author, title, subject, keyword, or even a library abbreviation to search the database. The display format of an individual bibliographic record can be customized to specifications.

Access to an individual title can take from one to five seconds. Considering that the disk contains more than 270,000 titles and provides subject and keyword searching, this speed is quite amazing. Several LePac users got a chuckle at a recent conference when an automation consultant in the audience attempted to pin down Brodart's sales staff regarding response time for searching on LePac. He couldn't seem to grasp that in most cases LePac is so fast that response time is not even an issue.

Each library in the Finger lakes Library System now has a LePac. The catalog includes the holdings records of all libraries in the system, though a library can limit its search to any specific collection, including its own. We now require that libraries search all ILL requests on the LePac prior to sending the request to system headquarters. The number of ILL requests handled by our ILL Department has risen by about 50 to 75 percent since November 1986.

PLUSES AND MINUSES

Some of the good points of LePac include:

- powerful searching capabilities
- fast response time
- user friendliness
- easier to handle than fiche
- durability, hardware stands up under hard use.

Some negative points are:

- glitches in software that can cause long searching loops (some recent changes in software have eliminated much of this problem).
- problems with display of certain records
- summary screens that do not include full holdings information.

LePac players cost from $2,200 to $2,900, depending upon volume. Costs of producing laser disks depend on the size of the data base and whether author or subject authority is chosen. We estimate that each cumulation of our 270,000-title database will cost around $9,000. Copies of the physical disks run about $60 each.

We have found that our union catalog display on LePac is much superior to fiche, provides much enhanced access to our database than either our card union catalog or our in-house automated circulation control system, is easy for our member librarians to learn, and has laid the groundwork for exciting interlibrary loan options now being developed by Brodart. In fact, we have just reached agreement to serve as Brodart's first test site for their new interlibrary loan system. We expect that our member library LePacs will soon be linked electronically and that our yearly 18,000 intrasystem interlibrary loan requests will be handled without a slip of paper changing hands or being filed. ILL requests will be routed to owning libraries; appropriate statistics will be kept regarding usage; and we hope these will help us do some load levelling of requests electronically.

To date, our only questions regarding LePac deal with the durability of the equipment. During our first seven months, there was only one equipment failure. We reported the breakdown, and Brodart shipped a replacement within 24 hours. We intend to handle equipment repairs on a time and materials basis rather than to purchase a service contract, which would cost approximately $6,000.

I wish I could turn the clock ahead and see if I would be as positive about Brodart's services two to five years from today. One thing that I have learned about library automation though is that we should be happy if our decisions prove valid even for two years. Two years from today, various vendors will be offering products at prices that will make today's seem laughable. So far, we are happy with our two decisions to purchase services from Brodart. As a company, they are accommodating, fun to work with, and seem to be on the cutting edge of laser disk technology.

6

OCLC

Paul W. Crumlish

In order to make an informed choice of a bibliographic utility, library administrators must examine the characteristics of different sources of bibliographic information and services. Any such examination must certainly include OCLC—the first and one of the largest and best established utilities available.

As a librarian responsible for a library that has been using OCLC since it arrived in New York State in 1974, I've had long experience with both its strong and weak points. (I am not an employee of OCLC nor of the SUNY/OCLC network, although I have been active in the governance of both the New York State OCLC Network, as a member of the Network Advisory Committee [SONAC], and of OCLC, as a member of the OCLC Users Council.)

Back in "the good old days" (before OCLC), throughput time in my library was about a year, typical for a college library and shorter than for most university libraries. (This meant that about a year elapsed from the time a book arrived in the library until it reached the shelf.) There were elaborate systems to keep track of uncataloged material in this frontlog (the euphemism then current for backlog) to reduce the number of times material was purchased that was already owned but not yet cataloged. All this ended with OCLC. My library does most of its trade purchasing from a jobber, who ships once a week; that delivery arrives on Thursday, and by the following Thursday the cataloging shelves are generally bare. Our typical throughput time now, from the time a book comes in the door until it is on the new-book shelf, is 10 or 12 days. OCLC has substantially increased the effectiveness of my library by enabling me to put material in users' hands much more quickly. It has virtually ended inadvertent duplication of material owned but not cataloged.

Another major problem the bad old days was keeping track of uncataloged material in circulation. A librarian could not deny faculty members access to material just because it wasn't cataloged yet. But how do you keep track of uncataloged material in circulation? That problem has vanished. We can now promise faculty four-hour service on demand. If a book happens to be in processing, we tell the faculty member that in four hours the book will be cataloged with card and pocket. There is no longer a problem of circulating uncataloged material. For cataloging, the "good old days" are now.

ORGANIZATION

The three fundamental characteristics of OCLC's organization are at once its major strengths and its principal liabilities. These are its organization, its Online Union Catalog, and its telecommunications network.

OCLC is a membership organization. Its assets are owned by a not-for-profit educational corporation. Any excess of revenues from fees for services to its users over expenditures contributes to the capitalization of OCLC, and all the capital that it holds has been generated by fees paid by users. There are no stockholders to receive dividends, and the management of OCLC is accountable to a Board of Trustees, selected, in part, by the participating members through a regional and national governance structure.

OCLC does not have sales representatives to sell its products and services to new customers. Instead commercial vendor's employ representative to sell bibliographic services. They can be very useful in helping a university library staff make an effective presentation to the campus administration. On the other hand, they represent substantial costs to the for-profit vendor—possibly 20% of the cost of doing business—which must be recovered promptly.

The need to recover these high first costs very quickly gave rise to the problem of vendor abandonment. The marketplace is now served by the third generation of local online systems vendors; two earlier generations came into the market, made sales, recovered very substantial first costs, and then abandoned the market.

OCLC today offers virtually every product and service it has ever offered. Further, it regularly upgrades services as a policy insisted on by the membership. The principle generally accepted in the Users Council is that the expense of making a conversion is a legitimate cost to be shared by all members, as replacing less efficient service with a more efficient way of doing the same task benefits all users.

For example, OCLC is currently replacing its online serials control subsystem with the distributed SC350 serials control system. Data conversion is being done at no direct cost to those libraries that have holdings in the online serials subsystem, and they are paying only half the regular startup charge.

While the first cost of acquiring a local online system is very high, entrance into OCLC is very inexpensive. The first cost for a library using OCLC for cataloging via dial access is little more than the price of a personal computer and a modem, which can be under $1000, and $750 to SUNY/OCLC for profiling and training; the rest of the OCLC charges are for use of various services.

With a few exceptions, libraries do not obtain services directly from OCLC, but from networks. Some networks are state agencies, and some are participant organizations themselves. Four libraries outside New York State and 263 libraries within the state acquire OCLC service through SUNY/OCLC, a hybrid network run out of the Office of the State University of New York (SUNY) Central Administration but entirely funded by fees paid by participants. The network is responsible for providing member libraries with local training in the use of various services and documentation. Operational details such as telephone line installation and equipment maintenance are handled by the network, which also provides support services such as tape storage and extract services.

As networks are either membership organizations with priorities set by their members or state-mandated agencies with some sort of participant input, networks have been free to select their own levels of support. Not all networks are equal in the level of support they provide. At one extreme, some networks have made substantial investments of participants' money in acquiring hardware and providing direct bibliographic services of their own to users (although recently there has been a retreat by the two most radical networks from that position). At the other extreme are networks which offer a minimum of service to their users at the least possible cost.

By the nature of the organization and in response to advice from its members, SUNY/OCLC has maintained a middle course, keeping as its central mission the provision of services in support of members' use of the OCLC Online Union Catalog. Therefore, its first priority has been field support for use of the Online Union Catalog. This support includes hands-on training in Albany and information meetings around the state to update users on developments in OCLC services and the Online Union Catalog. As a consumer of SUNY/OCLC field services since 1974, I can testify to the consistent high quality of these services.

The cruel fact of network service is that libraries' heaviest demand on network staff is during initial start-up. After a library has been using the Online Union Catalog for a year or so, its ongoing requirement for training and support is fairly modest. Once the terminal has been installed and staff has received initial training, all that is needed is to keep up to date with changes and new services. On the advice of the Network Advisory Committee, SUNY/OCLC has maintained a fee structure that does not decrease as time goes on and the library's demand for network service diminishes. The aim of this policy is to make entrance into the OCLC system as easy as possible, thus encouraging additional libraries to join. The more libraries that participate in OCLC and contribute cataloging and holdings information to the Online Union Catalog, the more useful OCLC is to each member.

THE ONLINE UNION CATALOG

The heart of OCLC is certainly its Online Union Catalog, a database of over 15 million bibliographic records. About 12 million of these records were created by member libraries and about three million by national libraries including the Library of Congress, the National Library of Medicine, the National Agricultural Library, the National Library of Canada, the U.S. Government Printing Offices and the British Library. The database is growing at the rate of about 30,000 records a week. About 24,000 of these are contributed by participating members, and the other 6,000 are from national libraries.' The largest portion of the Online Union Catalog is monographs (about 85 percent); serials are about six percent (but a very important portion), and the balance is sound recordings, films, music scores, maps, archive manuscripts, and machine-readable data files. Seventy percent of material is in the English language, and the remaining 30 percent represents the distribution of Roman-alphabet languages one would expect. The Online Union Catalog also contains about a quarter of a billion holding statements.

There are over 6,000 libraries in the U.S. and 14 other countries using OCLC for cataloging and contributing cataloging. Overall, participating libraries locate bibliographic records for about 96 percent of the items they catalog each year and contribute their cataloging for about four percent of the items they add. This percentage varies by type of library. My library, an academic library serving an exclusively undergraduate institution, performs original cataloging for less than one percent of our new acquisitions, excluding archival material. Research libraries, on the other hand, which acquire exotic materials such as non-trade imprints and non-Roman alphabet material, have a different hit rate.

Use of the database for shared cataloging is the major benefit of OCLC participation. About half of OCLC's annual revenues come from the Online Union Catalog, principally through the first-time-use fee (FTU) that a participating member pays for the use of a pre-existing bibliographic record. Libraries do not pay for adding cataloging to the system; on the contrary, they currently receive a 50 cent credit for each original record they add. With the right to use the Online Union Catalog comes the responsibility to contribute to it. All full participant members assume responsibility for adding location holdings and contributing all original cataloging they do for current Roman-alphabet acquisitions.

A testimonial to the contribution that OCLC cataloging makes to my library is that after two years' use of the cataloging subsystem, two and a half FTE positions were transferred out from technical services into public services, where they were needed to meet increased demands for services resulting from a move into a new library building. At that time (1976), the direct annual cost of these positions was about $25,000, which was more than twice the cost of using OCLC for cataloging.

THE COMMUNICATIONS NETWORK

The third component of OCLC's organization is the communications system. When put together in 1972, OCLC's telecommunications network was far more ambitious than anything anyone else had attempted. Their dedicated-line 2400 baud communication system was on the cutting edge of technology, although it used what are, by today's standards, fairly stupid terminals. This dedicated-line system has in many ways served OCLC quite well. It required no technical competence on the part of member libraries (you just walked over and turned the terminal on). This dedicated-line network has proven quite reliable and has been cost-effective for libraries doing a significant volume of cataloging.

However, the fixed cost of the dedicated telecommunications network has been a major barrier to the use of the OCLC Online Union Catalog by smaller libraries. (At this time, the telecommunications cost for a single terminal on a dedicated line in New York State is about $3,200 per year.) Originally, the expense of cataloging fewer than 5,000 new titles a year by OCLC was not significantly less than traditional cataloging. Librarians acquiring fewer titles had to decide if putting books into people's hands more quickly was worth the additional cost.

There has recently been a significant increase in the number of librarians who communicate with OCLC via dial access instead of the dedicated communications network. Technological improvements have narrowed the gap in effectiveness between dial access and dedicated line access. OCLC provides software usable on virtually any compatible PC with the appropriate memory, graphics capability and modem. Dial access substantially reduces the cost to libraries that do not use their terminal the full 92 hours a week that online service is offered.

ADDITIONAL SERVICES

As OCLC began to amass this large database scale, it was obvious that more could be done with this aggregation of bibliographic data and the telecommunications network. The first new application was the Interlibrary Loan Subsystem. The Online Union Catalog contains both bibliographic descriptions and holding locations. The OCLC communications network is outstanding for its effectiveness (although not necessarily for its low cost), so the ILL subsystem was devised which allow librarians to place interlibrary loan requests using OCLC's dedicated-line communications network.

The ILL subsystem has proven to be a very important benefit to users. Over 3,100 libraries are now using it to send interlibrary loan requests to over 6,000 libraries that use the OCLC Online Union Catalog, and they average about 65,000 requests each week. The principal benefit of the OCLC/ILL system is that all requests are known-location, point-to-point requests. The requesting librarian has only to look in the Online Union Catalog to identify the bibliographic record of the item it wishes to borrow and up to five libraries that hold it. The designated libraries are queried electronically by the ILL system as to whether the item is available for loan. About 86 percent of the requests placed are filled, and, on average, the item is on its way to the borrowing library in four days.

My experience with the ILL subsystem has been a fill rate of 99.6 percent, not surprising at a four-year college where students are our major users. Our average turnaround time using the ILL subsystem is just a little over eight days, down from more than two weeks.

Although the ILL Subsystem has not substantially reduced our cost of operation, it has materially increased our ILL effectiveness. We pay 99 cents per request entered and receive 20 cents credit for each item we loan. These charges about equal the labor saved by eliminating paper records of ILL requests entered and multiple requests to different locations. The status of a request can be checked online, so the reference librarian can tell users if they are going to get their item, and when.

It is not necessary to be a full member of OCLC to use the ILL Subsystem. More smaller libraries are joining group access arrangements in which OCLC members agree to make their holdings available to non-members in a particular region. This has become important in New York State as the Rochester, Western New York, Central and Long Island 3R's Regions have gone together to create a group access arrangement. Non-OCLC libraries can place loan requests via dial access in the four regions and can even contribute their holdings to the Online Union Catalog. All they need is a PC of some sort, a modem and a telephone line.

THE BOTTOM LINE

As of this writing, the fixed cost in round numbers for a library using a single dedicated-line terminal for cataloging is just under $7,000 per year; adding ILL increases the fixed cost to about $7,500. A library cataloging 5,000 titles per year would incur about $6,000 in first time use charges and about $2,500 in card printing costs, for a total of $16,000, or just over $3 per title added. If the same library makes 1,000 ILL requests, costs would increase to about $17,500.

Offline Products

The OCLC Online Union Catalog has become an increasingly important source of bibliographic data for producing offline products. Originally with microfiche but increasingly with CD-ROM, there is an alternative to online access for libraries widely scattered and too small to justify the cost of even dial access. Both CD-ROM and microfiche are very attractive ways to distribute bibliographic data around a campus, to multiple locations, or branch libraries. Although theoretically a fine tool, there is general agreement that microfiche is universally detested by users.

However, CD-ROM provides a way to manipulate bibliographic data at a fairly reasonable cost and offers a level of sophistication in searching beyond that provided by the OCLC Online Union Catalog itself, including Boolean keyword access. An example from my region: five libraries in Ontario and Wayne Counties have been cooperatively adding their holdings to the OCLC Online Union Catalog. In 1985, using the archival tapes of our bibliographic data obtained from OCLC, we arranged with a third-party vendor, Brodart, to produce a CD-ROM Union Catalog of the holdings of the two academic and the three largest public libraries in our two counties. In 1986, bibliographic data from Brodart for the local school library system's holdings were included to produce a new edition of this two-county union catalog on CD-ROM containing over 240,000 unique titles and about 290,000 holdings.

Another direct use of the Online Union Catalog (OLUC) is union listing. Although only 6.2 percent of the bibliographic records in the OLUC comprises serials, we all realize that serial records have an importance far greater than their numbers would suggest. Library after library has passed that threshold where it spends as much for serials as for monographs. The Serials Union List Subsystem has permitted regions (in New York State, all nine 3R's regions) to put serials holdings of both OCLC participants and non-participants into the Online Union Catalog where it can be used for bibliographic verification, for interlibrary loan and for production of a local union list as an offline product for distribution to members.

At this time, OCLC provides offline products only on tape, paper, or microfiche. CD-ROM products derived from the Online Union Catalog are being developed. I certainly hope that soon librarians will be able to do one-stop shopping and acquire a CD-ROM local union list directly from OCLC. How soon this will happen is up to the members. If we make it clear to OCLC management that this is our priority, it will be done. If there is no consensus among members, it won't be done.

LOOKING AHEAD

What is the future of OCLC? As stated earlier, its three principal assets—that it is a membership organization, that it has an online union catalog of over 15 million items, and that its dedicated-line and dial-access communications network links over 6,000 libraries—are also its principal liabilities. As a membership organization, it reflects the priorities of its members. Therefore, libraries not previously able to afford OCLC services don't have effective representation in the setting of OCLC's priorities. Some members have a pull-up-the-ladder mentality that impedes development of cost-effective products and services of benefit to smaller libraries.

Nevertheless, there is some progress in developing new products and services. The CD-ROM cataloging package, in particular, promises to make the Online Union Catalog cost-effective for smaller libraries. OCLC plans to distribute a CD-ROM package that will contain 90 percent of the bibliographic records used by a typical single-terminal library. Libraries using this service would first search their own CD-ROM file and only go to the Online Union Catalog via dial access to search and bring down records for the 10 percent of their cataloging not on the disks, and to add their holding symbols to the OLUC. This could reduce costs by up to 40 percent for single-terminal libraries by reducing communications costs.

The principal liability of a 15-million-item database is that redesigning the database and methods of access to it are a monumental undertaking. OCLC has committed a major portion of its liquid capital to a redesign of both the communications network and the Online Union Catalog itself. Rebuilding the communications network is a long-term project with a multi-million dollar price tag. When OCLC was created there was no standard communications protocol for computer communications, let alone communication of bibliographic data. OCLC had to invent its own communication protocol, and as a result its network can only be accessed using proprietary OCLC terminals. For a number of reasons it is going to be cheaper in the long run to convert to a standard, synchronous, packet-switched network which will allow libraries a choice in how they communicate with OCLC.

The tools for accessing the Online Union Catalog are also being redesigned. (Originally called the Oxford Project, the redesign is now called the New System.) The purpose of the redesign is to improve efficiency by providing more powerful editing tools and more powerful access to bibliographic records. When OCLC first came to libraries in 1974, librarians were amazed at the ease and speed of editing bibliographic records. However, now that librarians have become accustomed to the power of word processing software, we find line-by-line editing tedious. The new system will provide full-screen editing, the kind we are accustomed to in word processing, as well as features such as windowing and block transfer of data from location to location within the Online Union Catalog and from other auxiliary online files such as name-authority files.

The new system will offer subject access to the Online Union Catalog, providing a search capability of the sort we now have come to expect through the use of online services such as BRS. It will also increase the effectiveness of database maintenance by providing utilities such as global changes in subject authority. Those who went through the previous *AACR II* conversion process know the importance of that.

Of greatest significance for resource sharing, the new system will display holdings online at whatever level of detail a library wishes to provide. The Online Union Catalog now displays holdings on the institution level only; it does not display exactly which library in a multiple branch system holds the desired item. When the new system is complete, a member will be able to include the holding library within the institution, holding collection within a library, or even parts of works, such as volumes of a multi-volume title.

However, converting the tools that support a database of over 15 million items is trivial task. It is going to take considerable resources and considerable time, particularly as it must be done without interrupting libraries' access to the Online Union Catalog.

The other major development in OCLC services is the increasing use of distributed processing. Current serials control subsystems and the acquisition subsystem are clearly interim measures. There are good reasons why the Online Union Catalog wants to know each time a participating library catalogs a new book. It provides cataloging information to all other member libraries so that they need not duplicate work that has already been done. It is also useful for the Online Union Catalog to know when a participating library adds a copy of a book, as that identifies another potential location for borrowing.

However, there is no reason why the Online Union Catalog needs to keep track of each issue of periodicals received by members nor the status of each member library's departmental book accounts. Therefore, both of these subsystems are being converted to microcomputer-based systems that will be free-standing in each library yet will be interactive with the Online Union Catalog. Bibliographic data will be brought from the Online Union Catalog by the micro-based system, and holdings will be sent back to it. Not only will this improve the efficiency of the system by reducing traffic in and out of the Online Union Catalog, but it will also improve the local library's operating efficiency. Since editing will be done locally, the time delays entailed in communicating back and forth to Columbus will be eliminated.

Clear trends in OCLC costs have emerged in the past several years. Unit costs of OCLC services have been consistently decreasing. The first-time-use charge has gone down 10 cents since 1984 (a 7.8 percent decrease); the ILL request charge has decreased 27 cents since 1983 (a 21.4 percent decrease). On the other hand, dedicated-line telecommunications charges continue to increase, which has spurred redesign of the network and development of services to make dial access more effective.

Charges have been redistributed to encourage responsible use of the database. I have already mentioned the 50-cents-per-title credit for contributing original cataloging to the Online Union Catalog, and the 20-cents credit for each ILL request filled. A charge for more than four searches per item and a charge for displaying holdings have also been introduced. I have yet to incur a charge for searching, and I doubt that any librarian making responsible use of the database would incur major search costs. As for the charge for displaying holding locations, my charges have been less than the credits earned by my library for filling ILL requests.

7

General Research Corporation: LaserQuest

Anne H. Chaney

Old Colony Library Network (OCLN) is a group of 21 public libraries, ranging in size from tiny to medium, all sharing an automated system and a single bibliographic database. When conversion is complete, the shared database should contain 500,000 bibliographic records with 1.3 million holdings. When OCLN began to actively seek a retrospective conversion vendor, the major considerations were: efficiency, cost, and utilizing a single method or vendor.

There were several low-cost options readily available, but they offered only LC monographic records or, alternatively, all LC records, which would give us, at most, 65 to 70 percent of the needed bibliographic records. Sources offering non-LC records, including pre-1968 imprints, were clearly beyond our budget. After further consideration, the Network decided to subsidize the five largest libraries for a four-month period of high-speed, high-productivity retrospective conversion.

First, the Network issued a request for proposals inviting bids on both offline and online services. We chose GRC's LaserQuest for its relatively low cost, high efficiency, and, most important, database size and depth. GRC had 20 years of experience in catalog conversion and more than four million bibliographic records in its database. LaserQuest is a compact-disk-based, stand-alone system. It consists of a compact disk drive, its interface cable and controller board, the database on four compact disks, and software to run the system. The system cost about $4,800, with an additional annual fee of $2100 for quarterly updates of the database.

As Network Coordinator, I ordered all equipment and supplies and handled installation of equipment, assembling of profile information, training of initial users, and panic calls. Each of the five libraries agreed to allocate a minimum of 35 staff hours per week to the project, while the Network subsidized the equivalent of an additional FTE in each library for the project period. In this way, LaserQuest systems could be maximized.

The process involved searching a title from shelflist or book in hand against the LaserQuest database. Upon locating and displaying a match, the user enters local information including call number, collection code(s), and bar code label number(s). Since barcode label numbers are unique, the majority of libraries decided against entering copy numbers. After briefly verifying data entry, the user saves the record to a floppy. Full disks are sent off to GRC to be processed onto a tape.

At this point, there are probably two issues uppermost in the reader's mind: what our hit rate was and average records per hour.

GRC had guessed that OCLN, as public libraries, should expect a hit rate of 99 percent. At first, when I received reports of 88 to 93 percent, I was somewhat disappointed. As users became more experienced, however, and professional staff began to check no-hits, the hit rate improved to 99 percent. One library, in fact, reported a 102 percent hit rate for awhile because they were finding most of the earlier no-hits. We have successfully located a large number of 19th-Century imprints in the database. To date, we have not attempted to convert the rare book and genealogical collections, but tests have revealed a 50 percent hit rate on these specialized materials.

We did not elect to have GRC perform re-duplication on the records since the Network's online software has this capability. When the tape output from GRC was loaded into OCLN's database and the work of five libraries was merged, the many duplicates in the GRC database did cause an ongoing quality control problem. Obviously, this would not present the same problem for a single-library conversion. Quality of non-LC records in the database varies widely from very brief records to full *National Union Catalog* transcription. As a cataloger, I find egregious the entries of four fields with the note "large type edition" appearing as the subtitle.

GRC reported that their experienced users could achieve 100 records per hour. We set a goal of 60 records per hour, but found this was ambitious. With many and various users in five libraries, averages range from 18 to 70 per hour, with an overall average of 50 per hour. Because it took so long to train all these assorted users, and even longer before they attained some level of expertise, it was two months into the project before this average could be established.

Even the experienced user bogs down when doing such sections as the Thomas Hardy in fiction, with its large number of editions and older materials. In many libraries, a conversion method like LaserQuest is the staff's first exposure to automation, and so we thought that as many staff members as possible should be "exposed." Considering our goals and the time frame of the project, this was naive. A user who gets onto the system one hour per week will probably never pass beyond the need for hand-holding and will yield very low productivity.

The next two questions that arise are: How difficult is Laser-Quest to learn? And are CDs really that fast?

CDs really are that fast. Even with the entire database available on four (or five) compact disk drives, the average search takes one second because the software knows exactly where each portion of the database is residing. Typical of any database search is that long lists of hits take much longer to process. The list of hits is displayed as matches are found, however, so that the user can begin to analyze results very quickly. Considering the size of the software program, most system functions are also very fast. For example, the SAVE function uses about two seconds to save the entire record, including validation.

Training on LaserQuest is somewhat of a problem. While the software is extremely helpful, most novice users want and need more guidance and must be encouraged to depend upon the online HELP and prompts. The LaserQuest manual is also variable in quality. Some sections are excellent, for example, that on system set-up and installation; others are rather ambiguous and should be improved. GRC has recently released a "quick-reference" index to the LaserQuest manual which has improved access to information. Customer-support staff is knowledgeable and patient, but the three-hour time difference can be frustrating. Unfortunately, most of our emergencies seemed to occur at 8:30 A.M.

As with most library projects, a manager should be designated to monitor system use, progress, and training, to insure consistency and productivity. In the one library without a clearly designated project manager, there was chaos for the first six weeks. All five project managers found it necessary to draft a simple manual outlining basic system use and local practices. Before instruction on LaserQuest, novice users should be encouraged to go through an introductory tutorial on using a PC.

The software is truly impressive. To date, we have only a few complaints on what is still a fairly new program. When a search yields only one match, the user must still enter the DISPLAY command to view the record. This is corrected in the supplement disk, but functions only when the supplement is loaded. The supplement also provides a split-screen display of multiple hits showing those derived from the original database and those from the supplement.

Users at OCLN would like to have a software check for "bad" diskettes. Because bad diskettes are infrequent, we did not address this problem at the outset, which resulted in about 30 to 40 hours of wasted work among the five libraries. Disks can be checked using the MS-DOS CHECKDISC function, and we now recommend that users periodically run the CHECKDISC command on diskettes. We also recommend making back-up copies as a standard procedure.

Once records are saved to a diskette, the task of checking, editing, and correcting them is cumbersome and poorly explained in the manual. I would like to see this function improved, although I suspect it is deliberately cumbersome to protect the work already saved.

Aside from these minor objections, GRC's software is sophisticated and impressive. Each record saved must pass through a number of checks built into the program. These include, for example, MARC tags and indicators and collection codes. Statistics on offline conversion projects give an average error rate of five percent. OCLN's error rate for the first tape output was less than one percent; for the second tape, two percent; the third is still waiting to be loaded. Considering the number of locations and people involved in the project, this error rate is impressively low; the reason is software validation features.

Another noteworthy software feature is the screen format and on-screen prompts. Once the user is comfortable with Laser-Quest, it will seldom prove necessary to refer to the manual, since each display contains a prompt line of functions specific to that display. The software can also guide the user through processes not often performed and, therefore, difficult to remember.

Later GRC added several new features to make LaserQuest even more efficient and easy to use. In addition to numeric MARC tags, a descriptive statement now appears to the left of each field, such as: Author 100 Adams, Alice. This allows effective use of LaserQuest without extensive familiarity with MARC tags. Users are now able to create and retain MARC templates for original entry. It is also possible to program the cursor position. Therefore, if local information is always entered following the last field, the cursor goes automatically to that position when a record is displayed. In addition, LaserQuest is now capable of supporting up to five readers, giving simultaneous access to the entire database and the supplement disk.

As stated earlier, efficiency was one of our major objectives. Efficiency is attained through fast software processing, very fast compact disk access, and keeping user keystrokes to a minimum. For example, the user may encode collection designations onto the numeric keypad. In the appropriate field and subfield, simply typing a number will cause the software to fill in the multi-letter collection designation. In addition, the user may also establish abbreviations for call number prefixes, for example, "mys" for MYSTERY. Each time the user enters "mys," the correct term MYSTERY will be substituted during tape creation.

PRC's support services have been extremely satisfactory. Typically, we made a few errors and omissions in the original profiles which GRC staff corrected cheerfully and efficiently. They have also dealt competently with panic calls, although some very strange problems have occurred. Our one complaint with GRC was in service on a defective compact disk reader. A 30-day turnaround on repair disrupted the project.

Would we choose LaserQuest again? Yes! LaserQuest has given us a cost-effective, efficient method of converting our holdings and access to a most extensive database. The goal for the project was 270,000 records in four months; we accomplished it in five months. We found, however, that the rate of duplication in collections was far higher than anticipated; after de-duplication, the online database had 145,000 unique bibliographic records. Will we continue to use LaserQuest for the remainder of conversion and for new acquisitions? Yes, again.

Users currently enter brief records for any item not located in the online database. These brief records are printed out and searched on LaserQuest. If a match is found, the record is saved to a floppy disk. Upon completing a batch, records on the diskette are run against a LaserQuest utility which translates them to MARC communications format. In this state, they can be downloaded directly to our online database. The hit rate continues to be 99 percent; for new acquisitions it's 80 to 85 percent. Items not located on LaserQuest are searched in OCLC. LaserQuest continues to be a most cost-effective medium for acquisition of bibliographic records.

Searches must be exact through the portion of the title entered, but matches with longer titles will be included in the list of hits; for example, the title *The Natural* by Bernard Malamud would be entered:

> natural
> ma

and might return such hits as:

TITLE	YEAR	PUB	PLACE	ED.	PAG	AU
The natural	1961	Doubled	US:NY	1st	261	Ma
The natural; a novel	1960	Simon &	US:NY		267	Se
Natural things; a play	1986	North P	US:CA	1st	177	Ma

but would not yield such hits as:

Naturalism	1959	Universe	US:PA		389	Un
The naturals; a play	1984	Random	US:NY	2nd		Ma

It is possible to limit searches by adding the subtitle and to expand searches through the use of "wildcards."

8

Blackwell North America (BNA)

Jeanne Somers

The Kent State University Library began planning for an integrated library system in October 1984, a process that would culminate in the decision to purchase NOTIS in September 1985. An important part of that process was a consideration of our database preparation needs. We had used OCLC since December 1971 and had amassed 53 institutional archive tapes containing 904,684 records. As the high record count suggests, we had converted our entire LC collection of Roman alphabet titles and so were in the happy position of knowing that our entire LC collection was in machine-readable form. Some other aspects of our situation were not so happy.

We knew that many of our early tapes had not been stored under ideal conditions, and we had some serious concerns about data loss. Verification (making sure that all 53 tapes contained data and that the data was readable) was one of our first priorities.

DUPLICATE RECORDS

Multiple use of the same OCLC record is common (to reflect cataloging revision, added volumes and added copies). Because each use (update/produce) of an OCLC record results in the creation of a separate archive record, if an institution is careful to recreate all local revisions, holdings statements, etc., in each subsequent use of a given record, it can rely on the latest use of that record to be authoritative.

Although we had been conscientious about reflecting correct call numbers and representing full, current holdings in the 049 holdings field every time we reused a given OCLC record, we had not consistently recreated bibliographic data in each subsequent use. We estimated that 15 percent of our archive records might be duplicates and knew that, because of inconsistent past practice, a standard latest-use edit would leave us with considerable local clean-up.

We were also aware that, although the OCLC database had been flipped in December 1980, all of the headings on our pre-1981 archive records would still be pre-*AACR2* forms. We anticipated the same rate of conflict in KSU records as had been predicted for the Library of Congress: personal names 10 to 15 per cent, corporate names 40 percent, geographic names 33 percent. We assumed there would be vagaries in our post-1981 input and production as well. There was no doubt that our archive records contained a variety of errors in MARC tags, subfield codes, and filing indicators, and we were hoping that a tape edit might correct a certain amount of this.

VENDOR SELECTION

General letters of inquiry were written to three of the major vendors of tape editing services—Amigos, BNA, and Solinet—asking them to describe the range of services they offered and to give cost information. All three offered roughly comparable verification and duplicate editing at a cost of approximately two cents per record. Although Amigos and BNA were willing to customize a dupe edit, cost and time constraints quickly pushed us toward accepting a standard, latest-use edit matching an OCLC record control number and keeping the record of latest use. We knew latest-use records would have correct and complete call numbers and holdings information. We intended to request a tape of the edited duplicates in order to deal with anticipated bibliographic problems in a separate local project.

AUTHORITY EDIT

The big difference among the three vendors was in the nature of the authority edit they offered. In the case of Amigos and Solinet, the 857,000 record tape which represented OCLC's December 1980 database flip (plus subsequent clean up operations through July 1981) served as the source file against which our bibliographic file would be matched. An edit of this kind would have addressed the problem of name authority only and, as far as we were concerned, addressed it rather inadequately. The BNA match constituted a true authority edit.

At the time of the Kent State project, the BNA authority database included approximately 370,000 subject authority records from LCSH ninth ed., and significant changes through the 1981 supplements. It also included commonly used names from the name authority file if appropriate for use as subjects. The name authority file contained almost 1,000,000 headings (the then current—March 1985—LC online authority file). BNA's name/subject authority edit was available at that time for ten cents per record. BNA could also provide authority record generation (i.e.. a full-authority record for each LC Name Authority file or LCSH match and a brief, no-cross-references record for KSU headings not matched) at a charge of one-quarter cent per record.

PROPOSAL

We deliberated about this information through the winter/spring of 1985/86, discussed with staff the various features we considered desirable and necessary, weighed them against costs, and formed a strong preference for the more complete BNA service. We then telephoned libraries of our size and type which had used BNA for tape editing and got uniformly positive responses.

During the fall of 1985, we prepared a document entitled "Database Preparation for NOTIS: A Proposal" in which we made our recommendation to contract for BNA tape editing services. This was approved by the director of libraries and the university administration. Since August of 1985, we had been working on a draft contract, which was formalized in terms of delivery dates and signed in December 1985.

THE PROJECT

Mishap

Kent State University Computer Services copied 57 tapes which were sent to BNA during the second week of December 1985. On December 19, BNA's sales and service manager called with some chilling news: at least 11 of our tapes were completely blank and his staff was having a hard time getting data off eight others. The Kent State Computer Services dumped the original tapes, found formatted data, and recopied readable versions for BNA.

Because this delayed the delivery of tapes to BNA, we revised deadlines and asked that our July-December 1985 archive tape of approximately 25,000 additional records be included. The new deadlines were: 100,000 test file March 1 (originally February 15), completed project June 30 (originally May 23).

Duplicate Edit

By the end of January, BNA had completed the dupe edit, reported that it had eliminated 177,335 duplicate records (18% of the original 961,113 record database), and delivered 12 computer tapes containing both the duplicates eliminated and the 106,940 latest-use records to which they corresponded—a total of 284,275 records on the duplicate tapes. This left 783,778 records in our bibliographic database eligible for authority edit. On the dupe tape provided by BNA, records were clustered by OCLC number and then arranged in reverse chronological order, by year, and in forward chronological order within year. Records with OCLC control numbers greater than 9,999,999 were clustered by OCLC number and appeared at the beginning of the tape in random order. The charge for creation of the KSU duplicate tape was $.007 per record. We planned to use the duplicate tape as the basis for a combination of machine and manual edits which would correct known problems related to multiple use.

Authority Edit

The headings in our bibliographic file were matched to the authority files at two levels: normalized form and catalog form. Headings were normalized in the following respects:

- All characters were set in upper case.
- Punctuation, diacritical marks, and special characters were removed.
- Spacing between words was regularized.

Then the normalized heading from the bibliographic file was matched to the normalized heading from the authority file.

After normalized forms were matched, a second match was done on the catalog form, which included MARC tags, indicators and subfield codes, full punctuation, capitalization, special and diacritical characters. If there was a difference between the Kent State heading and the authority file heading, the authority file form was assumed to be correct and replaced the Kent State form.

Both full and partial matches were possible based on a breakdown into the following record types: main heading, subdivision, see reference, and abbreviation.

A full match is self-explanatory, a one-for-one comparison. If the heading could not be matched in full, however, each of its parts (the main heading and the subdivision) was matched independently and recombined into a new legal heading. If an incorrect form appeared in our bibliographic file, it was matched to a cross reference in the authority file and converted to the correct form. In situations where an old form had split into more than one valid new heading, the system reported to an editor who inspected the bibliographic records and made the heading assignment.

Miscellaneous Edits

In the process of authority matching, the following additional problems were to be corrected: inconsistencies in spacing, punctuation, and capitalization; MARC tags and subfield codes; incorrect qualifiers; errors of inversion. Death dates were added to headings that lacked them, and changes were made from direct to indirect geographic subdivisions. As far as series were concerned, at the time of Kent State's project, only the 400, 410, 411, 800, 810, 811 were matched. BNA can now match 440 also.

THE PRODUCT

Quantitative Analysis

BNA delivered, on schedule, 57 tapes containing: 783,743 bibliographic records; 521,594 name authority records; 345,985 subject authority records.

The following additional statistics provide a summary of the volume and nature of the BNA edits:

	NAMES	SUBJECTS
Number of records	783,779	783,779
Number of headings	1,1764,432	1,216,416
Full match	528,477	797,814
Match on LC cross ref	78,280	21,665
Match on multiple cross ref	2,279	3,504
Match on supplement file	0	14,338
Non matches	415,525	79,317
Manual updates	146,145	68,436
Automatic updates	235,137	233,826
Automatic tag updates	1,021	9,304
LC authority records	162,475	215,389
Minimal lvl authority recs	183,510	306,205
Full match hdgs (after edit)	699,006	960,762
Non match hdgs (after edit)	383,683	59,634

Authority Loading Software

Although we had the BNA generated authority database in hand in July 1986, we were not able to load it until November. NOTIS software had been installed at the end of April, and by the end of June we had loaded a small test file of KSU bibliographic records. In September we attempted to put some authority records online and discovered a small problem. The 001 field of the BNA generated authority records contained either an LC ARON or a BNA number. In either case, the NOTIS authority loader was taking the B characters in position 4 through 11, adding an OCLC identifier and placing them in the 035 field. NOTIS corrected the problem, and in November we actually loaded our authority file.

Qualitative Analysis

At this writing, we have not yet loaded the bibliographic database. NOTIS is working on version 2 of our loading software, so no comment is possible on the results of the dupe edit. Our examination of the duplicate tape and our test file gives every indication that BNA did precisely what we asked for: perform a standard latest-use edit. We knew that our choice of this no-frills dupe edit would result in some incorrect bibliographic information. Although we have not yet loaded our bibliographic database, headings on bibliographic records in the test file appear to have been flipped correctly.

The authority file is, of course, in MARC format and contains the following categories of headings:

- those matched to LC authority data (LCSH, LC Online Authority File) including LC cross references deblinded according to the KSU bibliographic file;
- those LC derived headings not yet in the LC authority file or LCSH (i.e., headings found on LC bibliographic records which do not yet appear in LC authority files), which were transferred to the KSU authority file without cross references;
- KSU-derived headings (i.e., headings found on non-LC bibliographic records which do not appear in LC authority files without further validation or change, referred to here as skeleton records.

Among other notable characteristics of the BNA authority file are duplicate authority records for headings used as names and subjects. If a heading had been used as both a name and a subject in our bib file, two separate authority records were created with fixed field codes indicating which use (name or subject) was the basis for authority record generation. Of course, in these situations, if one record was a skeleton (for example, a heading generated by a subject use in a KSU bib record with no LC authority file match), it was less complete than its name-generated counterpart if that counterpart was represented by a full LC match.

However, even if both records were matches to the LC source file, they will routinely vary in content. In the example in Figure 1, both records bear the same LC ARCN. The first one, generated from a subject, lacks the second cross reference and the last 670.

This is not so much a problem as something we simply don't understand. Duplicates of this kind will be merged into a single authority record.

Figure 1

```
   LTKE  DONE                                              CAR6263
                                      NOTIS CATALOGING                T002
   KE‡ CAR6263 FMT A R/TYP z DT 01/13/87 R/DT none      STAT mn E/LEV n
   SRC   LANG      ROM    MOD   UNIQUE a GOVT   S/SYS a D/I n NUM n S/TYP n
   NAME a SUBJ c SER b AUTH a H/ESTAB a T/EVAL a IP a RULES c

   010:    : ‡a n  50050534
   040:    : ‡a DLC ‡c DLC
   100:10: ‡a Queneau, Raymond, ‡d 1903-1976
   400/1:10: ‡a Mara, Sally, ‡d 1903-1976
   670/1:   : ‡a His Gueule de Pierre ... 1934.
   670/2:   : ‡a His We always treat women too well, 1981: ‡b t.p. (Raymond
   Queneau, originally published under the pseudonym Sally Mara)

   LTKE  DONE                                              CBP5932
                                      NOTIS CATALOGING                T002
   KE‡ CBP5932 FMT A R/TYP z DT 01/13/87 R/DT none      STAT mn E/LEV n
   SRC   LANG      ROM    MOD   UNIQUE a GOVT   S/SYS a D/I n NUM n S/TYP n
   NAME c SUBJ a SER b AUTH a H/ESTAB a T/EVAL a IP a RULES c

   010:    : ‡a n  50050534
   040:    : ‡a DLC ‡c DLC ‡d DLC
   100:10: ‡a Queneau, Raymond, ‡d 1903-1976.
   400/1:10: ‡a Mara, Sally, ‡d 1903-1976
   400/2:10: ‡a Raymond, Jean, ‡d 1903-1976
   670/1:   : ‡a His Gueule de Pierre ... 1934.
   670/2:   : ‡a His We always treat women too well, 1981: ‡b t.p. (Raymond
   Queneau, originally published under the pseudonym Sally Mara)
   670/3:   : ‡a Quéval, J. Raymond Queneau, c1984: ‡b t.p. (Raymond Queneau) p.
   5 of plates (b. 2-21-1903 in Le Havre, d. 1976) p. 12 of plates (pseud.: Jean
   RAYMOND)
```

Other Types of Duplicate Records

Our own incorrect input has very often resulted in duplicate authority records. In the Holbrook example in Figure 2, the lack of a space before the forename warranted retention of a second authority record.

In the DeAngeli example, Figure 3, a KSU-derived skeleton which lacks a birthdate coexists with a full MARC LC authority record for the same individual.

Cases like DeAngeli (involving dates in personal names) occur because BNA, as a matter of policy, does not commit to adding or changing birthdates. No doubt such a policy maximizes accuracy in most headings. It seems, however, that manual editors might safely correct birth and death dates for famous people. The

Figure 2

```
LTKE DONE                                                   CCW3666
                                       NOTIS CATALOGING                0813
KE# CCW3666 FMT A R/TYP z DT 01/13/87 R/DT none
SRC u LANG ??? ROM ? MOD   UNIQUE ? GOVT u S/SYS n D/I m NUM ? S/TYP n
NAME c SUBJ b SER ? AUTH a H/ESTAB a T/EVAL n IP a RULES ?

035/1:   :  |a (BNA)001468966
100:10:  |a Holbrook,Stewart Hall, |d 1893-1964
```

```
LTKE DONE                                                   CBT2767
                                       NOTIS CATALOGING                0813
KE# CBT2767 FMT A R/TYP z DT 01/13/87 R/DT none      STAT mn E/LEV n
SRC    LANG     ROM    MOD   UNIQUE a GOVT   S/SYS a D/I n NUM n S/TYP n
NAME c SUBJ a SER b AUTH a H/ESTAB a T/EVAL a IP a RULES d

010:    :  |a n  79068384
040:    :  |a DLC |c DLC
100:10:  |a Holbrook, Stewart Hall, |d 1893-1964.
400/1:10:  |a Holbrook, Stewart H. |q (Stewart Hall), |d 1893-1964
400/2:10:  |a Holbrook, Stewart, |d 1893-1964
670/1:    :  |a His Holy old Mackinaw, 1938.
670/2:    :  |a His The story of American railroads, 1981: |b t.p. (Stewart H.
Holbrook) '
670/3:    :  |a His Green commonwealth, 1945: |b t.p. (Stewart Holbrook)
```

Figure 3

```
LTKE DONE                                                   CCD7938
                                       NOTIS CATALOGING                T002
KE# CCD7938 FMT A R/TYP z DT 01/13/67 R/DT none      STAT mn E/LEV o
SRC u LANG ??? ROM ? MOD   UNIQUE ? GOVT u S/SYS n D/I n NUM ? S/TYP n
NAME c SUBJ b SER ? AUTH a H/ESTAB a T/EVAL n IP a RULES ?

035/1:   :  |a (BNA)001413238
100:10:  |a De Angeli, Marguerite
```

```
LTKE DONE                                                   CBP3443
                                       NOTIS CATALOGING                T002
KE# CBP3443 FMT A R/TYP z DT 01/13/87 R/DT none      STAT mn E/LEV n
SRC    LANG     ROM    MOD   UNIQUE a GOVT   S/SYS a D/I n NUM n S/TYP n
NAME c SUBJ a SER b AUTH a H/ESTAB a T/EVAL a IP a RULES c

010:    :  |a n  50045743
040:    :  |a DLC |c DLC |d DLC
100:10:  |a De Angeli, Marguerite, |d 1889-
400/1:10:  |a Angeli, Marguerite De, |d 1889-
400/2:10:  |w nna |a De Angeli, Marguerite Lofft, |d 1889-
670/1:    :  |a Her Ted and Nina go to the grocery store ... 1935.
670/2:    :  |a LCCN 64-14812: Her The Ted and Nina story book, 1965 |b (hdg.: De
Angeli, Marguerite (Lofft) 1889-; usage: Marguerite de Angeli)
```

examples in Figures 4 and 5 from our file illustrate cases in which major headings might have shown more evidence of manual editing.

Deblinding

Deblinding was accomplished by coding of the fourth position (Ref Display/Print Restriction) of #w. Based on a match of x ref fields (4xx and 5xx) to the bibliographic database, the fourth position was coded either:

Figure 4

```
LTKE DONE                                          CBGB083
                                    NOTIS CATALOGING            0813
KE# CBGB083 FMT A R/TYP z  DT 01/13/87 R/DT none      STAT mn E/LEV o
SRC u LANG ??? ROM ? MOD    UNIQUE ? GOVT u S/SYS a D/I    NUM n S/TYP n
NAME b SUBJ c SER b AUTH a H/ESTAB a T/EVAL n IP a RULES n

035/1:   :  |a (BNA)000774812
150: 0:  |a Shakespeare, William, |d 1564-1616
```

```
LTKE MORE                                          CBR7439
                                    NOTIS CATALOGING            0813
KE# CBR7439 FMT A R/TYP z  DT 01/13/87 R/DT none      STAT mn E/LEV n
SRC    LANG     ROM    MOD    UNIQUE a GOVT    S/SYS a D/I n NUM n S/TYP n
NAME c SUBJ a SER b AUTH a H/ESTAB a T/EVAL a IP a RULES c

010:     :  |a n 78095332
040:     :  |a DLC |c DLC |d DLC
100:10:  |a Shakespeare, William, |d 1564-1616.
400/1:10:  |a Shakspeare, William, |d 1564-1615
400/2:10:  |a Saixp\-er, Gouilliam, |d 1564-1616
400/3:10:  |a Shakspere, William, |d 1564-1616
400/4:10:  |a Shikisb\-ir, Wilyam, |d 1564-1616
400/5:10:  |a Szekspir, Wiliam, |d 1564-1616
400/6:10:  |a \)Sekspyras, |d 1564-1616
400/7:10:  |a Shekspir, Vil\t\$i\&am, |d 1564-1616
400/8:10:  |a \)Sekspir, Viljem, |d 1564-1616
400/9:20:  |a Tsikinya-chaka, |d 1564-1616
400/10:20:  |a Sha-shih-pi-ya, |d 1564-1616
400/11:10:  |a Shashibiya, |d 1564-1616
400/12:10:  |a She\.kspir, \.Vilyam, |d 1564-1616
400/13:10:  |a Sha\.kspir, \.Vilyam, |d 1564-1616
```

```
LTKE DONE                                          CDJ4759
                                    NOTIS CATALOGING            0813
KE# CDJ4759 FMT A R/TYP z  DT 01/13/87 R/DT none      STAT mn E/LEV o
SRC u LANG ??? ROM ? MOD    UNIQUE ? GOVT u S/SYS n D/I n NUM ? S/TYP n
NAME c SUBJ b SER ? AUTH a H/ESTAB a T/EVAL n IP a RULES ?

035/1:   :  |a (BNA)001590059
100:10:  |a Shakespeare, William
```

n=the reference is displayed to the public, or
a=no reference is made or displayed to the public.

Of course, we will not see the impact of deblinding until NOTIS index redesign is implemented.

GENERAL SATISFACTION

Thus far, I can report a very high level of satisfaction with BNA's work. When we first noted what we thought were duplicate records resulting from errors in BNA's edit, we reported some initial findings to them and began systematically browsing the indexes for additional examples. In the process, we realized that there were actually very few cases in which BNA could be faulted. Their response confirmed that much of what looked like redun-

Figure 5

```
LTKE DONE                                              CBR9121
                                      NOTIS CATALOGING            081:
KE# CBR9121 FMT A R/TYP z DT 01/13/87 R/DT none     STAT mn E/LEV n
SRC    LANG     ROM    MOD    UNIQUE a GOVT    S/SYS a D/I n NUM n S/TYP n
NAME c SUBJ a SER b AUTH a H/ESTAB a T/EVAL a IP a RULES c

010:   :  |a n  79006779
040:   :  |a DLC |c DLC
100:10: |a Lincoln, Abraham, |d 1809-1865.
400:1:10: |w nnaa |a Lincoln, Abraham, |c Pres. U.S., |d 1809-1865.
400/2:10: |a Link\]uln, Abrakham, |d 1809-1865
400/3:10: |a Linkol\tn, Avraam, |d 1809-1865
400/4:10: |a Link\-uln, Ibr\-ah\-im, |d 1809-1865
400/5:10: |a Linkan, \,Abreh\-am, |d 1809-1865
400/6:10: |a Lincoln, A. |q (Abraham), |d 1809-1865
510:1:10: |a United States. |b President (1861-1865 : Lincoln)
670:1:   :  |a Schriver, L. O. Seven Lincoln shrines, 1947 (subj.)

LTKE DONE                                              CBB7729
                                      NOTIS CATALOGING            0813
KE# CBB7729 FMT A R/TYP z DT 01/13/87 R/DT none     STAT mn E/LEV o
SRC u LANG ??? ROM ? MOD    UNIQUE ? GOVT u S/SYS a D/I    NUM n S/TYP n
NAME b SUBJ c SER b AUTH a H/ESTAB a T/EVAL n IP a RULES ?

035/1:   :  |a (BNA)000724458
100:10: |a Lincoln, Abraham, |c pres. U.S., |d 1869-1865

LTKE DONE                                              CBB7734
                                      NOTIS CATALOGING            0813
KE# CBB7734 FMT A R/TYP z DT 01/13/87 R/DT none     STAT mn E/LEV o
SRC u LANG ??? ROM ? MOD    UNIQUE ? GOVT u S/SYS a D/I    NUM n S/TYP n
NAME b SUBJ c SER b AUTH a H/ESTAB a T/EVAL n IP a RULES ?

035/1:   :  |a (BNA)000724463
100:10: |a Lincoln, Abraham, |d 1800-1865

LTKE DONE                                              CBB7732
                                      NOTIS CATALOGING            0813
KE# CBB7732 FMT A R/TYP z DT 01/13/87 R/DT none     STAT mn E/LEV o
SRC u LANG ??? ROM ? MOD    UNIQUE ? GOVT u S/SYS a D/I    NUM n S/TYP n
NAME b SUBJ c SER b AUTH a H/ESTAB a T/EVAL n IP a, RULES n

035/1:   :  |a (BNA)000724461
150: 0: |a Lincoln, Abraham, |d 1809-1865

LTKE DONE                                              CBB7721
                                      NOTIS CATALOGING            0813
KE# CBB7721 FMT A R/TYP z DT 01/13/87 R/DT none     STAT mn E/LEV o
SRC u LANG ??? ROM ? MOD    UNIQUE ? GOVT u S/SYS a D/I    NUM n S/TYP n
NAME b SUBJ c SER b AUTH a H/ESTAB a T/EVAL n IP a RULES ?

035/1:   :  |a (BNA)000724450
100:10: |a Lincoln, Abraham, |c pres. U. S.

LTKE DONE                                              CBB7766
                                      NOTIS CATALOGING            0813
KE# CBB7766 FMT A R/TYP z DT 01/13/87 R/DT none     STAT mn E/LEV o
SRC u LANG ??? ROM ? MOD    UNIQUE ? GOVT u S/SYS a D/I    NUM n S/TYP n
NAME b SUBJ c SER b AUTH a H/ESTAB a T/EVAL n IP a RULES ?

035/1:   :  |a (BNA)000724495
100:10: |a Lincoln, Abraham, |d 1809-1965

                                      NOTIS CATALOGING
KE# CBB7735 FMT A R/TYP z DT 01/13/87 R/DT none     STAT mn E/LEV o
SRC u LANG ??? ROM ? MOD    UNIQUE ? GOVT u S/SYS a D/I    NUM n S/TYP n
NAME b SUBJ c SER b AUTH a H/ESTAB a T/EVAL n IP a RULES ?

035/1:   :  |a (BNA)000724464
100:10: |a Lincoln, Abraham, |d 1806-1865
```

dancy was simply a result of their policy *not* to add or change birthdates.

The random errors uncovered are negligible considering the size and quality of the Kent State database: 2,380,848 headings displaying a universe of input errors. It was our impression, during the six-month course of BNA's work, that the Kent State project was handled with the kind of meticulous care we had hoped for. For example, on several occasions BNA's service manager phoned with lists of obsolete headings now split into two or more new headings and asked us to check the pieces on the shelf in order to guide BNA in correct heading assignment.

Given the size and complexity of our file, local achievement of the same ends—de-duping, headings flip, authority record generation—would have been impossible. Attempting to bring up a database without such an edit would have resulted in chaos. We are confident that the work BNA did has given us an enormous edge in system implementation and will insure clearer access to the collection and, ultimately, greater user satisfaction.

9

Marcive Inc.

Eleanor Seminara

MARCIVE provides an inexpensive, rapid means of obtaining MARC records for any automation purpose. MARCIVE currently serves about 4000 libraries.

MARCIVE subscribes to and makes available the following MARC files:

Library of Congress—LC cataloging for monographs, serials, filmstrips and other AV material, maps and music. Includes COMARC, Books for College Libraries, and, optionally Cataloging in Publication (CIP). Most extensive coverage are years 1968 to the present, but LC continues to distribute thousands of pre-1968 records as well.

Government Printing Office—U.S. government document cataloging for monographs, serials, microforms, etc., from 1976 to the present.

National Library of Medicine—all NLM cataloging (CATLINE) for monographs, serials and other media material including AVLINE and retrospective titles from the NLM's history of medicine collection.

National Library of Canada—complete cataloging database.

All databases are updated immediately upon receipt of data from the cataloging agency. The library has access to records six to eight weeks faster than it would from a static source such as CD/ROM.

Some book jobbers provide MARC records, but unless the jobber uses MARCIVE to provide this service, they do not retain a copy of the library's database for remote backup. But MARCIVE (and any jobber which uses MARCIVE) retains a copy of all of the library's MARC record orders. The library submits lists of "search access numbers" usable by the MARCIVE system. These access numbers include ISBN, ISSN, GPO, NLM, and LC card number.

These lists may be submitted in any of the following ways:

1. Transmit search access numbers in MARCIVE 65-character format directly from a microcomputer using MARCIVE Electronic Mailbox.
2. Transmit search access numbers using MARCIVE's Cataloging Input System microcomputer software.
3. Transmit search access numbers directly from a participating integrated system vendor (Examples of systems which transmit search access numbers and accept MARC records in return: Dynix, Sydney Data Products, SIRSI, The Assistant, Scribe, Data Trek.)
4. Mail a magnetic tape (800 bpi or 1600 bpi) of search access numbers in MARCIVE 65-character format.
5. Mail a diskette of the search-access numbers using MARCIVE's Cataloging Input System software.
6. Mail a paper list of typed or handwritten search access numbers in MARCIVE 65-character format or mutually agreeable alternative.
7. Arrange with the library's book jobber to transmit search access numbers automatically to MARCIVE for each book order; our participating jobber is Taylor Carlisle. A listing of jobbers is available in theMARCIVE Literature.

MARCIVE compares the library's list of search access numbers against its master database and a match (or "hit") will result in the retrieval of the full cataloging record. A list of "no hits" (MARC records that are not yet available) will be produced.

The library may receive the "hits" (bibliographic records found) in one of the following ways:

1. MARC magnetic tape (800 bpi or 1600 bpi);
2. diskette in standard microcomputer transmission format;
3. direct transmission into a system whose software can read MARC records.

The library may create original cataloging records for any "no hits" directly on its local automated system. However, this means that those records exist only on that system. MARCIVE offers a way to create a library-specific MARC database and keep a backup copy of every cataloging order placed through the following methods:

1. *Cataloging Input System* (CIS)—MARCIVE microcomputer software which permits ordering of standard and supplemented cataloging and creation of original cataloging.

2. *Original Cataloging Input* (OCI)—MARCIVE worksheet method of creating original cataloging records.
3. *Mitinet/MARC*—Information Transform software (502 Leonard St., Madison, WI 53711) which permits creation of original cataloging.

These records are output along with standard hits.

Bibliographic records from MARCIVE can be customized to individual library requirements. Deletion or modification of specified records or specified fields within records can usually be done at no additional cost. Addition of constant or certain computable fields to all records is also available. MARCIVE also offers a subject authority control system.

A library can have all subject headings in its cataloging records verified against the file of Library of Congress Subject Headings, ninth edition, plus selected revisions. By signing up for the MARCIVE automatic authority control, a library can have all topical and geographic subject headings either verified as current authoritative forms, or as earlier obsolete forms and updated. Even common punctuation and some spelling errors are corrected. If a heading cannot be identified as either current or obsolete, it is left unchanged, but a report is created to alert the librarian to its presence.

As an optional part of the MARCIVE authority control processing, the library may choose to have "see" and/or "see also" cross-references created while its bibliographic records are being manipulated. Because the cross-reference generation is done at the same time as the bib records themselves are being examined, it is possible to de-blind all references and eliminate any duplicates. The resulting cross-references are mainly intended for use in a MARCIVE produced COM (microfilm or microfiche) catalog, but they can also be supplied on magnetic tape in a format similar to the MARC Authorities format.

Many local integrated systems or circulation systems have software which permits the library to type in search access numbers. The system then transmits these numbers to the main MARCIVE computer. The numbers are searched overnight to locate matches according to the library's profile. The librarian instructs the system to dial the main MARCIVE computer and "pick up" the bibliographic records which were found. The system captures the records, indexes them, and makes them immediately available to users of the system.

In many areas of the country, both of these transmissions (uploading search access numbers and downloading MARC records) are toll-free. There is never a connect charge.

Some of the systems which already have a link to the economical MARCIVE MARC Record Service:

- Sydney Dataproducts. Los Angeles, CA (1-800-992-9778)
- Dynix, Inc. Provo, UT (801-375-2770)
- Sirsi. Huntsville, AL (205-881-2140)
- Data Trek, Inc. Encinitas, CA (619-436-5055)
- Library Automation Products (The Assistant). New York, NY (212-967-7440)
- Scribe Software. Tucson, AZ (602-990-3384)

The Cataloging Input System (CIS) is a software package for:

- Standard Cataloging (ordering cataloging using LCCN, ISBN, Citation Number, or other access number)
- Supplemented Cataloging (ordering cataloging using access numbers, but supplemented with local notes or other information)
- Original Cataloging (creating original cataloging whenever appropriate cataloging is unavailable by access number)

CIS is a program that allows you to order standard cataloging using an IBM/PC (or compatible) microcomputer. The program is not copy protected. There is no longer any need to establish a work processing file for ordering and wonder if you have it set up properly. CIS knows the MARCIVE format.

The automated search request form is easy to fill in and easy to review for errors. It helps avoid common ordering mistakes. No special symbols are needed for upper and lower case. CIS takes your call numbers and locations exactly as you type them.

CIS is a program which allows you to use the special MARCIVE "A/B" format to order supplemented cataloging on your IBM/PC. You would use this option when you believe standard cataloging is basically appropriate but you need to add special local information. You simply type in the search access number (for example, LCCN) and follow it with the extra fields (a local subject heading, a holdings note, or any other supplemental information you need on your cataloging). These local fields are inserted into the proper position on your cards and MARC records.

CIS also allows you to create original cataloging records on your IBM/PC. The system asks you to fill in labeled "data entry boxes." You can go back and edit the record as many times as you like. No need to use the standard red-lined forms (and no more striking out lines of cataloging and starting over just because you ran out of room).

Using CIS is preferable to typing catalog cards, not only because it is easier but because a computer (MARC format) record is created and stored for every title. This means you will not have to perform a retrospective conversion in the future. You may send a diskette copy of the CIS cataloging files to MARCIVE or transmit the files over telephone lines.

You can use CIS with your modem and communications software (such as Hayes SmartCOM or compatible, 1200 baud setting) to create files of cataloging orders and original cataloging and transmit those files into the MARCIVE computer. For those of you in areas served by the MARCIVE WATS line, there is no charge for telecommunications.

No one pays a connect fee and, best of all, the cataloging products are produced within a few hours of your transmission. CIS can also be used for retrospective conversion. If you keep a copy of your diskette, you can edit existing bibliographic records to create cataloging for new editions, or it can be used to create and maintain cataloging records for a MARCIVE COM catalog.

You can create original cataloging records in MARC format on CIS, transmit (or mail) the records to MARCIVE, and then have MARCIVE transmit them down into your local circulation system. (Your original records are safely stored in two places--your system and MARCIVE's.)

CIS was designed for easy of use. Familiar terms are used throughout the system. The software is accompanied by documentation that explains every feature of the system and includes many examples, an index, and a glossary.

CIS can be used with either MARC numeric or MARCIVE alphabetic tags. In fact, the system permits moving back and forth from one type of tag display to the other. Either way, the records created are in true MARC format.

CIS requires the hardware and operating system most libraries already have: a microcomputer which is 100 percent compatible with the IBM/PC, a 25 line x 80 character display monitor, and a floppy disk drive. The operating system must be MS/DOS or IBM/DOS 2.0 or higher.

WHAT IT DOES FOR US

Niagara County Community College accesses the MARCIVE database through our book jobber. We mail order forms to them, and they send information to MARCIVE for cataloging data. The MARCIVE database is accessed by search access number, which is generally the ISBN, ISSN, LCCN, GPO or NLM number. Our jobber does all the work involved in obtaining the ISBN, filling out the forms and matching the card sets with books. If the wrong card set is generated due to an incorrect ISBN, then the jobber returns it and handles the credit memos. All we receive from the jobber is an invoice for correct card sets. When we receive the book, the card sets are shipped in the same package so matching the book with its card set is easy. We also receive three labels that are packaged with the card set. A card set and labels cost us about one dollar.

The cards themselves are die-cut, conform to ANSI Standard Z85.1 and are computer printed using the American Library Association type font. Pressure-sensitive, foil-backed labels with the call number and a portion of the author and title for check out cards and pockets are sent. We also receive a spine label with just the call number.

MARCIVE stores our cataloging information on magnetic tape in standard MARC format for no additional charge. If the title we request is not yet in the MARCIVE database, we receive the book without cataloging. However, the MARCIVE computer stores our request and when the cataloging data appears from the Library of Congress, for example, that record is loaded into our database at MARCIVE. Cards and labels are not generated by Marcive for these subsequent hits. Cataloging is obtained from UTLAS or created inhouse for those items.

We have uploaded our MARCIVE data into UTLAS very successfully. We had fewer errors than from data loaded from OCLC. Tape costs, as with all MARCIVE products, are very economical. In the past we have paid $25 for the tape and five cents for record loaded. We have found the MARCIVE hit rate to be about 82 percent. Many of the no hits are for books with incorrect ISBN numbers.

There is a disadvantage to not having online access to data. When our files were uploaded, we found about four percent of the entries had to be changed primarily due to our choices of alternate call numbers. Some titles cataloged in Reference turned out to be circulating materials, and those changes had to be done item by item.

We are in the process of considering a broad range of library automation packages, products, and processes. Ideally, we want a system that is an integrated in-house system for a public access catalog, for online circulation, for cataloging, for online ordering and for serials check-in. We now have about 30 percent of our bibliographic records for book materials in a COM catalog from another supplier. Serious consideration will be given to the MARCIVE COM product.

In pulling together information about the new MARCIVE offerings for this report, we realized that MARCIVE has made great strides in library automation, particularly for economical products for small institutions. Most interesting is the Public Access System that uses an updatable Compact Disc. MARCIVE supplies both hardware and software. We see this system as an example of a way to permanently reduce connect and hit charges, which can overwhelm a small institution.

10

Auto-graphics' Agile

Diana Cunningham

Choosing a bibliographic utility is simple in theory, but incredibly complex in practice. Throughout the decision-making process the desired end result must be kept in mind. The Maryland Division of Library Development and Services chose Auto-graphics' AGILE system because it best met our specific objectives. Although AGILE offers many features, we only use functions that support our state's overall goal: to improve resource sharing among Maryland libraries.

Our project plan included five objectives. The AGILE system features supporting those objectives are: bibliographic search and verification; online interlibrary loan; database management; statistical management data; and multiple uses at local option. The project was called MILNET to describe our specific application of the AGILE system.

THE MILNET SYSTEM

MILNET incorporates an online bibliographic database management system with an online interlibrary loan/electronic mail component. Communication with the mainframe UNIVAC host computer in California via AT&T leased longlines transmitting data at speeds of 4800-baud from 13 local microcomputers. Although microcomputers are not required, each Maryland site was equipped with a Sperry PC, model 20 with 128K memory and 2320K floppy disk drives, a Data South, 132-column, 180-cps dot matrix printer, and a synchronous 4800-baud modem to access the system. Major system functions include electronic mail, interlibrary loan, switch (terminal to terminal communication), and database search and maintenance (change, add, delete).

OBJECTIVES

1. Timely Bibliographic Verification and Identification

Our first objective was flexibility in searching and identifying bibliographic records from multiple access points.

MILNET's database was built on current Maryland State Union Database records. As of July 1986, our monographic union catalog, published in COM format, included approximately 1.6 million unique titles and 3.3 million holdings for more than 60 libraries of all types throughout Maryland. However, our agreement limited the state to records published since 1968. Analysis of statewide interlibrary loan activity indicated that requests for such materials comprised the bulk of interlibrary loan activity. The current file of more than 900,000 records is available online.

Access to the older, static file continues through COM. This ensures that magnetic tapes from various sources including vendors, utilities, and in-house systems can be merged or added to the current file on a monthly basis to reflect new holdings and titles of contributing libraries. Monthly tape loading means users can verify and access more up-to-date titles from more comprehensive holdings. Analysis shows an average of 15,000 new titles and 72,000 new holdings were added each month to the online database.

Online access to the MILNET database is available by author, title, keyword in title, Library of Congress Card Number (LCCN), International Standard Book Number (ISBN), record control number, subject, or combinations of these data. Searches can also be qualified by imprint data or data range, material format, and/or Boolean operands. Subfields of subject headings are also indexed. A full MARC record can also be displayed. A typical basic search sequence would reveal the results shown in Table 1.

2. Faster and more efficient

MILNET includes a sophisticated electronic mail/interlibrary loan system. Once a record is located in the database, bibliographic data and pertinent holdings information can be automatically transferred to an ILL request form. From holdings associated with the record, the system constructs an automatic referral schedule. Users establish their own defaults for data and batches responses, prints all incoming requests on individual forms with a single command, and provide status reports on command. In addition, ILL request files are indexed by author, title, patron name or number, as well as ILL request number. Books and serial items not in the database can be keyboarded using a blank ILL work form. A special reference request form was also developed for the system. Sample screens follow Table 1.

Table 1: Title search

```
FIND TTL=OF MINNIE THE MOOCHER AND ME,ATH=CALLOWAY
```

```
FIND TTL=OF MINNIE THE MOOCHER AND ME,ATH=CALLOWAY
  DSP 000319668,,MNETM   TTL=OF MINNIE THE MOOCHER AND ME
                         ATH=CALLOWAY CAB
                         PUB=Crowell
                         LC#=75-045160   DATE=c1976
```

MARC RECORD

```
SEGMENT JUST SEARCHED YIELDED THE ABOVE MATCH(ES).
SEARCH COMPLETE.
DSP ,000319668,,MNETM
-FIELD-- IND ---CONTENTS---------BK LOCATED IN YOUR MASTER FILE        04/23/85
  HLD.1        $1 ANNE $a 780.921 Calloway
  HLD.2        $1 BCPL $a B C
  HLD.3        $1 PRGE $a 780.92 Calloway
  UDB.1        $c 4
  008.1        000000n*********xx*************00000*und**
  010.1    **  $a 75-045160
  020.1    **  $a 690-01032-X
  100.1    10  $a Calloway, Cab, $d 1908-
  245.1    10  $a Of Minnie the Moocher and me, $b by Cab Calloway and Bryant ····
               Rollins; with ill. selected and edited by John Shearer.
  260.1    0*  $b Crowell $c c1976
  300.1    **  $a 282p   ill
  650.1    *0  $a Calloway, Cab, $d 1908-
```

```
END OF DISPLAY
```

Table 2: ILL work form

```
                                                          REQ.IYPE!AT
    REQ.DATE!042385 NEED BEFORE!072285    REC.DATE!       SHIP!       STATUS!REQ
    RET.DATE!          DUE DATE!      NEWDUE DATE!      RENEWREQ!   B.BRO-ER!PRAT
    REFERRALS!BCPL(99)!PROE(99)!ANNE(99)                           BORRO-ER!PRA.
                           SUBSTITUTE!N PHOTOCOPY!N CCG!  CCL!  AUTHORIZED BY!
    AUTHOR!CALLOWAY CAB
    TITLE!OF MINNIE THE MOOCHER AND ME

    IMPRINT!Crowell c1976            EDITION!
    PATRON!CEN CUNNINGHAM              VERIFIED!AGILE II

    ARTICLE!
    VOL!               NO!              DATE!            PGS!
    NOTES!



    LOCATION!BCPL B C
            PROE 780.92 Calloway
            ANNE 780.921 Calloway
```

Table 3: ILL batch update

```
    ILL CHG,SRQ       DEFAULTS: SHIP=041885 DUE=052885            04/18/2-
      REQ. #   SHIP    DUE LENDER           NOTES           ERROR
    ------    -----   ----- ----  --------------------------  -----------------
    L4873
    L4647
    L4815
    L4663
    L4648
    L4670
    L4616
    LDONE
    L
    L
    L
    L
    L
    L
    L
    L.
    L
    L
    L
    L
    L
    BATCH UPDATE COMPLETED.
    ILL DSP,L004616           CURRENT STATUS:SENDING REQUEST
    REQ.DATE:041685 NEED BEFORE:061485    REC.DATE:      SHIP:041885 B.BROKER:BCPL
    RET.DATE:  — — —  DUE DATE:052885 NEWDUE DATE:— — —  RENEWREQ+ —  BORROWER:BCPL
                         SUBSTITUTE:N PHOTOCOPY:N CCG:    L.BROKER:PRAT LENDER:PRAT
    AUTHOR:THERESE                                    CCL:  AUTHORIZED BY:
    TITLE:STORY OF A SOUL

    IMPRINT:ICS PUBLICATIONS, C1976.   EDITION:2D ED.TEDO
    PATRON:LR                            VERIFIED:AGILE II
    CALL NO:BX4700.T3 A5 1976
    ARTICLE:
    VOL:               NO:              DATE:            PGS:
    NOTES:
```

Table 4: Borrower status report

```
ILL DSP,L000662                     CURRENT STATUS:IN PROCESS
REQ.DATE:040285 NEED BEFORE:062085    REC.DATE:        SHIP:        B. :ROKER:ANNE
RET.DATE:              DUE DATE:     NEWDUE DATE:        RENEWREQ:    BC:ROWER:AN:E
REFERRALS:PRAT/NRQ(99):PRGE/NRQ(99):HARF/   (99):TSCO/   (99):SLRC/   (99)
                         SUBSTITUTE:N PHOTOCOPY:N CCG:  CCL:  AUTHORIZED BY:
AUTHOR:GRAY HENRY
TITLE:GRAYS ANATOMY

IMPRINT:SAUNDERS, 1980.            EDITION:36TH ED. /
PATRON:MOYER T (RIV)              VERIFIED:AGILE II
CALL NO:
ARTICLE:
VOL:            NO:              DATE:              POS:
NOTES:PRAT EXT(X)QM23.2G73G,PRGE 611G,HARF 611.G,MONT 611.01G779A,WEL: 0S4.0779R
A,UMHS QM23.G7B      1200 MEADOWVIEW ROAD   21122   255-1431


LOCATION:TSCO Ref. QM23.2.075 1980
        CACO REF QM23.2.073 1980
        EBCC QM23.073 1980
        JHUE UGL QM23.2.073 1980
       +JHUE UGL REF QM23.2.073 1980

END OF DISPLAY.
```

Table 5: Lender status report

```
ILL DSP,L000212                     CURRENT STATUS:SENDING REQUEST
REQ.DATE:031985 NEED BEFORE:051785    REC.DATE:        SHIP:032585 B.BROKER:PRAT
RET.DATE:              DUE DATE:041585 NEWDUE DATE:     RENEWREQ:    BORROWER:PRAT
                                                        L.BROKER:BCPL LENDER:BCPL
                         SUBSTITUTE:N PHOTOCOPY:N CCG:  CCL:  AUTHORIZED BY:
AUTHOR:GOULD STEPHEN JAY
TITLE:EVER SINCE DARWIN

IMPRINT:NORTON, C1977.            EDITION:
PATRON:CEN COHEN                 VERIFIED:AGILE II
CALL NO:575.0162 G
ARTICLE:
VOL:            NO:              DATE:              POS:
NOTES:




END OF DISPLAY.
```

3. Ongoing maintenance and updating of the state union database

Under our agreement, the Bibliographic Control Center at the State Library Resource Center (Enoch Pratt Free Library) monitors the updates, improves the database quality control, and performs both bibliographic and holdings maintenance using the cataloging (CAT) and holdings (HLD) functions. Additions, corrections, and deletions are performed by the Center on an item-by item-basis. Automated withdrawals or application of local catalog "kill tapes" are coordinated by the Center. Table 7 shows an example.

Table 6: Reference

```
ILL DSP,L001164                      CURRENT STATUS:SENDING REQUEST
REQ.DATE:032585 NEED BEFORE:062385    REC.DATE:      SHIP:040885 B.BROKER:ANNE
RET.DATE:            DUE DATE:051885 NEWDUE DATE:     RENEWREQ:    BORROWER:ANNE
                                                     L.BROKER:PRAT LENDER:PRAT

PATRON:TYLER G (SCO)                              PHONE NO:867-0372
ADDRESS:4846 RIVERSIDE GALESVILLE 20765

QUESTION:PATRON HAS A PAINTING SIGNED BY IVANOVITCH KOWALSKI AND WOULD LIKE TO K
NOW MORE ABOUT THE ARTIST AND ABOUT THE VALUE OF THE PAINTING.  THE PAINTING IS
AN IMPRESSIONIST WORK OF SMALL SAILBOATS IN THE SUNSET.  THE NATIONALITY OF THE
PAINTER IS UNKNOWN.  THE PAINTING WAS ACQUIRED RECENTLY BUT IS THOUGHT TO BE FRO
M THE LATE 19TH C.
MATERIAL USED:DICT. OF AMERICAN ARTISTS, SCULPTORS, AND ENGRAVERS--YOUNG, FIELD
ING DICT. OF AMERICAN PAINTERS, SCULPTORS, AND ENGRAVERS, DICT. OF CONTEMPORARY A
MERICAN ARTISTS--CUMMINGS, PHAIDON DICT. OF TWENTIETH CENTURY ART, NEW INTERNATI
ONAL ILLUS. ENCY. OF ART, CONTEMPORARY ARTISTS-- NAYLOR, MCGRAW-HILL ENCY. OF WO
RLD ART, BIOGRAPHICAL INDEX 46 - 84, WHO'S WHO IN AMERICAN 84 - 85

NOTES:SENDING 1 PHOTOCOPY FROM BENEZIT.


END OF DISPLAY.
```

Table 7: Tape loading information

```
E
ela read,show0082                                                04/10/8:
  To Pat Wallace: The OCLC, RLIN, EPFL OCLC, and Baker & Taylor records have all
been loaded as of. last night 4/10/85.  OCLC cancels to records cataloged in the
last three quarters of 1984 have been applied.  Those which cancel records cata
oged earlier remain to be applied. There were a total of 2192 cancels.  The foll
owing is a summary of record counts from the processing of the files loaded.

                OCLC Quarterly          RLIN/EPFL/BIT          TOTAL
INPUT           222575                  119353                 341929
AFTER OCLC DDUP  146199                  ------                  ------
GE 1968          93791                  82374                  176165
MATCHED BY LC    34984                  34933                   69917
TO TEXT MATCH    58807                  47441                  10624J
MATCHED BY TEXT  (Files had been merged at this point)          33057
NEW ACC ADDED    .............................................  73191

LC NUMBER MATCHES 69917
TEXT MATCHES       33057
NEW ACC ADDED     +73191
------------------------
                  176165

I will let you know when the next batch is loaded. Steve Rowley
```

Seeing records online showed that the database had many quality control problems. Because of the variant (some say vagrant) sources of our records, many titles could not be merged using the routing automated match program. The AGILE system supports a merge function that collapses like records which fail the automated match criteria. This has been an extremely powerful database maintenance tool. Following is an example of split record entries for the same item:

Table 8: Split record entries

```
fnd ttl=unobtrusiveON
  DSP 000978431,,MILON    TTL=UNOBTRUSIVE MEASUREMENT TODAY
                          PUB=Jossey-Bass,
                          LC#=78-073929  DATE=1979.
  DSP 000300371,,MILON    TTL=UNOBTRUSIVE MEASURES
                          ATH=WEBB EUGENE J
                          PUB=Rand McNally
                          LC#=66-010806  DATE=c1966
  DSP 000939389,,MILON    TTL=UNOBTRUSIVE MEASURES
                          PUB=Rand McNally
                          LC#=66-010806  DATE=[1966]
  DSP 000852009,,MILON    TTL=UNOBTRUSIVE MEASURES NONREACTIVE RESEARCH IN THE
                                 SOCIAL SCIENCES
                          ATH=WEBB EUGENE J
                          PUB=Rand McNally
                          LC#=66-010806  DATE=[1966]
```

Split records can be merged easily using AGILE's merging command. Table 9 illustrates this feature.

Although the bibliographic Control Center has full password access to change and merge bibliographic data, all sites can add, delete, or correct their own holdings. A library that continues to get requests for an item it no longer owns can remove holding data immediately online. Holderless records in the file are purged annually.

4. Reports of Interactive Network use for Management

AGILE supports two types of statistical reports: database and interlibrary loan performance data. Routine online database statistics include: number of records loaded (batch); number of records changes made; running total of online masterfile records; manually produced database update statistics.

In addition, statistical reports are also provided including: number of holdings from each contributing library; record counts by quality group; record counts by number of holdings attached to each title; field counts; record counts by publication year.

Table 9: Merging split records

```
~rg 040470068,040635236
 DSP 040470068,,MNETM  TTL-MOTHERS CAN DO ANYTHING
                       ATH-LASKER JOE
                       PUB-A. Whitman
                       LC#=72-083684  DATE=[1972]
 DSP 040635236,,MNETM  TTL-MOTHERS CAN DO ANYTHING
                       ATH-LASKER JOE
                       PUB-Whitman
                       DATE-1972


   E
DSP 040470068,,MNETM
-FIELD-- IND --CONTENTS---------BK LOCATED IN YOUR MASTER FILE        02/20/87
  HLD.1         $r ESRL $1 KENT $a 331.4/3/0973
  HLD.2         $r XXXX $1 BCPL $a E
  HLD.3         $r XXXX $1 HARF $a EL
  HLD.4         $r XXXX $1 HOWA $a E La
  HLD.5         $r XXXX $1 PRGE $a E Fic
  VNB.1         $c 4
  008.1         ??????$1972$$$$iluo$$$j$$$$$$00110$eng$$
  010.1    $$   $a 72-083684 /AC
  020.1    $$   $a 0807552879
  043.1    $$   $a n-us---
  050.1    0$   $a HD6055 $b .L33
  082.1    $$   $a 331.4/3/0973
  100.1    10   $a Lasker, Joe.
  245.1    10   $a Mothers can do anything. $c Words and pictures by Joe Lasker.
  240.1    0$   $a Chicago, $b A. Whitman $c [1972]


DSP 040470068,,MNETW
-FIELD-- IND --CONTENTS---------BK LOCATED IN YOUR WORK FILE         02/20/87
  HLD.1         $r ESRL $1 KENT $a 331.4/3/0973
  HLD.2         $r XXXX $1 ANNE $a JP
  HLD.3         $r XXXX $1 BCPL $a E
  HLD.4         $r XXXX $1 HARF $a EL
  HLD.5         $r XXXX $1 HOWA $a E La
  HLD.6         $r XXXX $1 PRGE $a E Fic
  DUB.1         $c 4
  008.1         ??????$1972$$$$iluo$$$J$$$$$$00110$eng$$
  010.1    $$   $a 72-083684 /AC
  020.1    $$   $a 0807552879
  043.1    $$   $a n-us---
  050.1    0$   $a HD6055 $b .L33
  082.1    $$   $a 331.4/3/0973
  100.1    10   $a Lasker, Joe.
  245.1    10   $a Mothers can do anything. $c Words and pictures by Joe Lasker.
  260.1    0$   $a Chicago, $b A. Whitman $c [1972]
  300.1    $$   $a [40] p. $b illus. (part col.) $c 23 cm.
  350.1    $$   $a $5.50
  520.1    $$   $a Text and illustrations demonstrate many occupations of mothers
                including plumber, dentist, subway conductor, and others.
  650.1    $1   $a Mothers.
MORE. PRESS XMIT TO CONTINUE.
DSP 040470068,,MNETW
-FIELD-- IND --CONTENTS---------BK LOCATED IN YOUR WORK FILE         02/20/87
  650.2    $1   $a Occupations.
  650.3    $$   $a Women $x Employment.
```

The decision to split the database at 1968 was based on an ILL use sample coupled with a detailed sort of the state union database by year and by holding code.

System-generated statistical reports of interlibrary loan performance data were developed according to our specifications. It is probably the most comprehensive program available. AGILE provides both MILNET or aggregated system totals, as well as individual site reports identifying who borrowed what from whom. Turnaround times are reported from both borrower and lender points of view if a request was not filled. Monthly and year-to-date data are reported, giving the state performance data about the network never before available. For example, turnaround times and point-to-point activity were never fully known.

Our FY 1986 report revealed that MILNET handled 76,147 requests from borrowers and successfully filled 52,755, for an overall online system fill rate of 69 percent. This, of course, does not include non-MILNET or brokered activity from the remaining 300-plus network participants. Author/title request accounted for 89 percent of all requests. Serial requests totaled slightly less than eight percent, and the balance was reference requests. Public libraries submitted most of the requests and have fill rates generally exceeding the overall state average.

Turnaround times for requests were very carefully defined. On average, a borrower can expect six to nine days to get a fill reported. Two sites, however, routinely report record turnaround times of one day each. The system cannot count less than a day! Unfilled status takes longer because the request continues from site to site until the "do-not-send-later-than" date has expired. Nevertheless, unfilled response times ranged between 15 and 22 days system-wide. Generally, the system required 1.35 tries to get a fill reported.

Examples of some of the detailed data routinely reported shown in Tables 10 and 11.

Table 11 shows by category why a request could not be filled. The major reason is that the material is in circulation. The second major reason for *not* filling a request is that the item was not owned in the first place. It should be noted that many of these unfilled requests were later filled by another site, or were resubmitted as a new request. MILNET is not using AGILE's reserve function feature. In sum, the data provided by Auto-graphics' AGILE system is an important management tool and is certainly a milestone for network performance data and analysis.

5. Multiple Local Options and Cost Effective use Equipment

The literature is ripe with arguments that automating interlibrary loan alone is not cost-effective; in fact, interlibrary loan may not be cost-effective at all. Although not required by the system, AGILE supports IBM PC-compatible equipment and

Table 10: MILNET turnaround times

GARODING MILKNET DIV (PTALS TURNAROUND TIMES FOR FILLED REQUESTS   JANUARY , 1987

FILLED REPLIES THIS MONTH

LENDERS — DAYS ELAPSED

LENDERS	01	02	03	04	05	06	07	08	09	10	11	12	13	14	15	16	17	18	19
ANNE																			
BCPL																			
MXRF																			
MOJA																			
MONT																			
PRAT																			
PRGE																			
TSCO																			
URBC																			
URCP																			
ESRL																			
SMRL																			
WMPL																			
SLRC																			

LENDERS — DAYS ELAPSED 20 21 22 23 24 25 26 27 28 29 30 +31 +61 +91   AVG   TOTAL

BORROWING ACTIVITY - OVERALL TURNAROUND TIME

FILLED REPLIES THIS MONTH

DAYS ELAPSED

TOTAL	01	02	03	04	05	06	07	08	09	10	11	12	13	14	15	16	17	18	19
TOTAL																			

DAYS ELAPSED

TOTAL	01	02	03	04	05	06	07	08	09	10	11	12	13	14	15	16	17	18
TOTAL																		

AVG   TOTAL

Table 11: Reasons reported for not filling requests as of June. 1986

Unfilled Reply Category	Last Mo's YTD	%	Current YTD	%
Item not in collection (NIC)	11542	23%	12431	23%
Item not available-in circulation (NAV)	30447	61%	32888	61%
Item not for loan (reference, etc.) (NRQ)	3714	7%	3988	7%
No response received (NRP)	107	0%	119	0%
Reserve (not possible) (NRS)	0	0%	1	0%
Need before date expired (NOX)	4063	8%	4331	8%
Total No. Unfilled Tries Reported	49873	100%	53758	100%
Total No. Unfilled Requests Reported			23392	

```
Total number of requests:          76147
Total number of filled requests:   52755
Total number of unfilled requests: 23392
```

software. Off-the-shelf software like DBase III and Lotus can easily be used. Libraries are encouraged to use the terminals for other purposes once interlibrary loan needs are met. Several sites are using the microcomputers for reserve lists, general reports, etc. In all counts under the five objectives, the AGILE system for MILNET was the system of choice.

EXPERIENCES WITH THE VENDOR

Adopting AGILE and creating MILNET fulfilled at least 10 years of trailblazing toward an online interlibrary loan network system. Vendor support at all levels was crucial. Auto-Graphics had been our COM vendor for more than 10 years, and their commitment to continue to develop and enhance an online database was solid. They were as interested in refining their online AGILE product as we were in tailoring it to our objectives. We saw developing the additional software as a shared responsibility and a mutual benefit. The essential software was developed according to our specifications and in a reasonably timely fashion.

The software enhancements were numerous. The system needed to recognize brokered activity on behalf of other sites. A reference form had to be developed. With high volumes of activity, operators found batch updating was essential to cut staff time. Function keys needed to be programmable. And because of numerous equipment and telecommunication problems, swap out arrangements were also needed. The vendor responded on all counts. Auto-Graphics also purchased diagnostic system equipment and assigned new personnel to staff a trouble desk. The vendor established an 800 number to Pomona, California, in response to our concern about downtime.

Developing software has proven to be time-consuming and expensive. Perhaps the most difficult software to develop was the system-generated performance statistics. It took at least two years just to define turnaround times.

Because of the numerous "vagrant animals" (sub-MARC data) in the database, much discussion and negotiation related to improved match criteria. Since the MILNET database was viewed as a finding tool, not a cataloging resource, quality codes were revised for source tapes and less stringent match criteria were developed. Edition statements, for example, created havoc when they were not uniformly included on source tapes. Many records also did not have properly subfielded subtitles which, under our old criteria, forced a split record to appear to the computer.

Interesting new possibilities have emerged. Negotiations with a vendor are never static. Now that we have information on unfilled requests by category, the state is investigating a diagnostic software package that will provide ILL request data down to the call number level. This project is currently begin negotiated.

Perhaps the best way to judge a vendor and a system is by comments of system operators themselves. A survey completed in February 1987 showed that MILNET system operators gave Auto-graphics extremely high marks. Most said the vendor's response to local problems was excellent. One respondent noted that the Auto-graphics staff was always "great, prompt, courteous, helpful and not condescending." Equipment performance was rated very good to excellent by 100 percent of respondents. Overall, the operators reported in glowing terms the larger percentage of new titles identified using the system, the sharp decreases in turnaround times, the reduction of staff time spent processing requests, and a decrease in error rates. The system also, by and large, eliminated staff time spent processing statistics. Some paper files were eliminated. Some reported staff time had been "drastically reduced in terms of bibliographic searching and the typing of requests."

Some sites reported adding staff to handle the increased request volume or due to an elevation of the ILL status to a service function which, under our guidelines, mandated a top priority for daily ILL services and responses. All sites have become "policemen" of sorts expecting all other sites to report status on a daily basis. One site did use the statistical report to do job performance ratings for the ILL staff. Their chief complaint was the limited number of sites on the system and their despair over maintaining the non-automated referral system. In fact, operators must maintain two systems: online and offline. The comments all reveal that the operators were in full support of the vendor and the system.

The relationship between the state and Auto-Graphics has been strengthened by our extensive, at times exhausting, experience developing MILNET. Our emphasis on performance objectives has provided the crucible for the state, the system, the sites, and the vendor to work as a team to make the project a continuing success. In fact, a new sense of interdependence has developed. The results speak for themselves.

11

AFLI

Paul Pugliese

The Association for Library Information (AFLI) was formed exclusively to contract services and products with Online Computer Library Center, Inc. (OCLC). According to AFLI's constitution and bylaws, the membership of the Association will be no less than three and shall be limited to academic, public, school, special, and governmental libraries. The only authority, rights, or obligations that accrue to a member in the association stem exclusively from the association's contract for OCLC services. All members of the association receive all letters, memorandums, technical bulletins and reports, publications, and other communications from OCLC. In addition, all members of the association may purchase any or all services and products offered by OCLC. In return, AFLI, as a cooperative, performs the administrative, training, support and marketing functions necessary for all members to receive OCLC services and products. AFLI is a full-service, single-purpose, unincorporated organization.

GETTING STARTED

The impetus that lead to the formation of AFLI began in 1978, when a few directors of libraries affiliated with the Pittsburgh Regional Library Center (PRLC) began to seriously question the increased cost of supporting the PRLC operation. After nearly three years of unsuccessful attempts to persuade the PRLC membership of the necessity to control costs, a group of concerned library directors met to discuss the situation. The dilemma was how the libraries could continue to pay for increasing network overhead costs described as necessary for conducting business when the directors were being asked by their parent institution or board of directors either to cut their library budget or to accept little or no increase at a time when the rate of inflation was increasing.

After discussing several alternatives, a choice was made in early 1981 to cooperate as an association of libraries and to request that OCLC enter into a contractual agreement to continue to provide online library services and products through the association to member libraries. On August 1, 1981, AFLI became operational. The underlying principles of this cooperation were and still remain the following:

1. Each participating institution in the cooperative venture must benefit.
   a) each institution has a responsibility to itself and its constituency that is prior to its responsibility to another institution or constituency.
   b) benefits can take many forms—added services, savings, improved quality—but should never be reduced to the to the "benefit of appearing to be cooperative."
2. Cooperation is a voluntary act. Each institution continues to control its own destiny. Ultimately this means that it retains the right, and has the duty, to withdraw if cooperative efforts are not successful according to its own judgement from its own criteria.
3. Successful cooperation must take into account the legitimate ambitions, as well as the present status, of the individual cooperating institutions.

Library directors joined AFLI in order to purchase OCLC services and products at the cheapest possible cost. AFLI's only purpose is to market and provide support for OCLC services and products. The current cost to AFLI member libraries purchasing services and products are the OCLC network cost plus 1.25% additional fee added to all invoices for supporting the overhead of providing copies of all memos, brochures, bulletins, correspondence, postage, supplies, telephone and travel. There is no annual membership fee. Five years ago our service fee was 2%, four years ago it was 1.5%, and effective 1984 it became 1.25%.

AFLI consists of 16 library member organizations: 11 are academic libraries; four are public libraries; and one is a special library. Of the 16 member libraries, nine are from Pennsylvania, three are from Ohio, and four are from Michigan.

While AFLI has no full-time paid employees, the executive director does attend OCLC network coordinators meetings, business managers meetings, users council meetings as a guest, Oxford Project Meetings, and other OCLC meetings as deemed necessary. All member libraries of AFLI receive prompt billing of activities and are encouraged to consider additional OCLC services and products. When necessary, OCLC staff are contracted for their usual fee, to conduct demonstrations of products such as the LS/2000 integrated library system and ACQ350. At times, AFLI arranges to send a group of staff from member libraries to OCLC for on-site demonstrations and discussions of products and services. The cost of sending a group is born by the member library.

AFLI is a small organization and an effective one for its members giving them the opportunity to purchase OCLC services and products at the lowest possible cost. Low overhead costs are possible in a group like AFLI because there is no interest in having all member libraries support projects and programs that benefit, in the main, a few members. If a member library wishes to purchase OCLC services and products, requires specialized training, or desires additional information or marketing support, then AFLI provides the opportunities. The full costs of these services and products are recovered from each member institution.

Since the beginning of AFLI's existence, the experience of all the directors and other staff of member AFLI libraries has been enriching and rewarding. There can be no doubt that my colleagues are articulate, informed about technological advances, and very much interested in OCLC services and products. All of the people involved have made AFLI function successfully and have made my job a pleasure.

However, not everyone has had a "love affair," as the saying goes, with AFLI. Executive directors of other networks became very concerned about AFLI's existence from the very first day. Their concern was well-founded because library directors now had an alternative to purchasing OCLC services and products, resulting in a loss of revenue to the former network. While a network may be able to tolerate or absorb the loss of one or two library accounts, network directors feared that a mass defection to AFLI could cause financial collapse. In many networks, library directors pay a high direct price for OCLC services and products. Total average mark-up costs in some networks have been as much as 16 to 20 percent, and some products have had much higher increases.

The first attempt to close down AFLI began as soon as it became a reality. Some network directors believed that AFLI could be written out of existence by developing criteria that would define a network. The attempt collapsed because the networks were dissimilar and it became apparent that not all of the criteria could be uncritically applied to every network.

The second attempt to close down AFLI began soon after two libraries from the Michigan Library Center (MLC) joined AFLI to purchase OCLC services and products. The renewed concern about AFLI's existence prompted many network directors and their staff to openly demand that OCLC put AFLI out of business or collaborate with them to put AFLI out of business. However, it soon became clear that OCLC could not engage in these activities because of possible charges of restraint of trade, price-fixing, and geographical restrictions.

The latest ploy is to separate networks into "full-service" and "less-than-full-service" categories. But what does "full service" and "less than full service" mean? Depending upon the definition, there may very well be few "full service" networks currently affiliated with OCLC. It is apparent that those network directors who use the term "less than full service" are suggesting that if such networks were to continue they would be damaging to OCLC programs, damaging to OCLC standards, and damaging to OCLC/Network relations. AFLI has rejected such suggestions. The evidence is clear that our quality of cataloging is excellent, that we support OCLC programs, and that we can and do market OCLC services and products.

CURRENT DEVELOPMENTS

AFLI has met the needs of member libraries since its inception. If has grown at a reasonable pace. The potential for expansion is tremendous, because there continue to be constant inquiries from all types and sizes of libraries. For AFLI, the future looks bright.

Contributors

Anne H. Chaney is Administrator, Old Colony Library Network.

Paul William Crumlish is Librarian, Hobart & William Smith Colleges, Geneva, NY.

Diana Sinclair Cunningham is Assistant Director, Information Services, University of Maryland Health Sciences Library.

Maurice J. Freedman is Director, Westchester Library System, NY.

Beverly Harris is Chief, Technical Services, Westchester Library System, NY.

Sally A. Knight is Coordinator, Cattaraugus-Allegany School Library System, NY.

Leslie Morris is Director of Libraries, Niagara University, NY.

Richard Panz is Director, Finger Lakes Library System.

Paul J. Pugliese is Director, University Library, Duquesne University, Pittsburgh, PA.

Phoebe Ruiz-Valera is Head of Technical Services, Association of the Bar of the City of New York.

Sherrie Schmidt is Head of Technical Services, Texas A&M University Libraries.

Eleanor Seminara is Director of the Library, Niagara County Community College, NY.

Jeanne Somers is Assistant Director, Head of Technical Services, Kent State University Library, OH.

John Zwick is Director of Learning Resources, Virginia Beach Campus, Tidewater Community College, VA.

Bibliography

Annual Review of OCLC Research, July 1985-June 1986.
OCLC Online Computer Library Center, Inc., Dublin, Ohio.
(ED278397)

Avram, Henriette D.
Current Issues in Networking. Journal of Academic Librarianship; v12 n4 p205-09 Sep 1986

Avram, Henriette D.; Wiggins, Beacher
The Role of the Linked Systems Project in Cooperation and Resource Sharing among Libraries.
Journal of Academic Librarianship; v13 n2 p100-A-D May 1987
Libraries and Computing Centers: Issues of Mutual Concern;
(Supplement) n2 p100a-100d May 1987

Baldwin, Paul E.; Swain, Leigh
RECON Alternatives for Eight British Columbia Public Libraries: An Ancillary Report for the British Columbia Library Network Prepared at the Request of the Greater Vancouver
Library Federation and Greater Victoria Public Library.
British Columbia Union Catalogue, Richmond.
ISBN-0-919093-04-3
1980
(ED200207)

Bearman, Toni Carbo
Library Networking: Current Problems and Future Prospects!
Resource Sharing and Information Networks; v1 n1-2 p87-98
Fall-Win 1983

Beaumont, Jane
Retrospective Conversion on a Micro: Options for Libraries.
Library Software Review; v5 n4 p213-18 Jul-Aug 1986

Berglund, Patricia
School Library Technology
Wilson Library Bulletin; v60 n8 p38-39 Apr 1986

Bidd, Donald; And Others
Computerized Information System Operates for A-V Materials.
Canadian Library Journal; v41 n6 p323-30 Dec 1984

Bishoff, Liz
Managing Technical Services in the Small Library.
Library Resources and Technical Services; v29 n2 p118-24 Apr-Jun 1985

Boss, Richard
Retrospective Conversion: Investing in the Future.
Wilson Library Bulletin; v59 n3 p173-78 Nov 1984

Boss, Richard W.
Technology and the Modern Library.
Library Journal; v109 n11 p1183-89 Jun 15 1984

Brown, Georgia L.
AACR2: OCLC's Implementation and Database Conversion.
Journal of Library Automation; v14 n3 p161-73 Sep 1981

Brown, Rowland C. W.; And Others
The Ownership of Bibliographic Data—OCLC's Experience: A Symposium.
Journal of Academic Librarianship; v11 n4 p196-205 Sep 1985

Campbell, Brian
Whither the White Knight: CDROM in Technical Services.
Database; v10 n4 p22-40 Aug 1987

Chen, Ching chih
Libraries in the Information Age: Where Are the Microcomputer and Laser Optical Disc Technologies Taking Us?
Microcomputers for Information Management: An International Journal for Library and Information Services; v3 n4 p253-65 Dec 1986

Cole, Elliot; McCain, Katherine W.
Adoption and Adaptation in the Use of Transaction Processing Systems: The Case of OCLC Software.
Information Processing and Management; v21 n1 p27-34 1986

Coty, Patricia Ann
The Status of Audiovisual Materials in Networking.
Special Libraries; v74 n3 p246-53 Jul 1983

Cribbs, Margaret A.
The Invisible Drip...How Data Seeps Away in Various Ways.
Online; v11 n2 p15-16, 18-26 Mar 1987

Cuadra, Carlos A.
The Local Electronic Library: Science Fiction or the Real Future?
Electronic Library; v1 n4 p257-64 Oct 1983

DeGennaro, Richard
Library Automation and Networking: Perspectives on Three Decades.
Library Journal; v108 n7 p629-35 Apr 1 1983

Dodd, Sue A.
Toward Integration of Catalog Records on Social Science Machine-Readable Data Files into Existing Bibliographic Utilities: A Commentary.
Library Trends; v30 n3 p335-61 Win 1982

Ford, Joseph
Network Service Centers and Their Expanding Role.
Information Technology and Libraries; v1 n1 p28-36 Mar 1982

Genaway, David C.
Microcomputers as Interfaces to Bibliographic Utilities (OCLC, RLIN, etc.).
Online; v7 n3 p21-27 May 1983

Hafter, Ruth
Born-Again Cataloging in the Online Networks.
College and Research libraries; v47 n4 p360-64 Jul 1986

Jones, Barbara; Kastner, Arno
Duplicate Records in the Bibliographic Utilities: A Historical Review of the Printing versus Edition Problem.
Library and Technical Services; v27 n2 p211-20 Apr-Jun 1983

Hoffman, Ellen
Library-Vendor Relations: An Era of New Challenges.
Canadian Library Journal; v44 n2 p89-92 Apr 1987

Jones, C. Lee
Linking Bibliographic Data Bases: A Discussion of the Battelle
Technical Report.
Council of Library Resources, Inc., Washington, D.C. 1980
(ED195274)

Juneja, Derry C.
Quality Control in Data Conversion.
Library Resources and Technical Services; v31 n2 p148-58 Apr-
Jun 1987

Kemp, Elaine; And Others
A Comparison of OCLC, RLG/RLIN, and WLN.
Journal of Library Automation; v14 n3 p215-30 Sep 81

Kennedy, H. Edward
Information Delivery Options over Three Decades.
NFAIS Newsletter; v28 n2 p31-47 Apr 1986
(ED274365)

Koenig, Michael E.D.
Information Systems Technology: On Entering Stage III.
Library Journal; v112 n2 p49-54 Feb 1 1987

Kruger, Betsy
NELINET: A Case Study of Regional Library Network Develop-
ment.
Information Technology and Libraries; v4 n2 p112-21 Jun 1985

Library Networking: Current Problems and Future Prospects!
Panel Discussion.
Resource Sharing and Information Networks; v1 n1-2 p99-139
Fall-Win 1983

Luthin, Patricia
Cataloging Marketplace.
Library Hi Tech; v1 n2 p53-62 Fall 1983

Lynch, Mary Jo
Information Technology, Library Management, and OCLC.
Information Technology and Libraries; v4 n2 p122-29 Jun 1985

MacDonald, R.W.
British Columbia Library Network. Final Report: Phase 1 Implementation.
British Columbia Library Network, Vancouver 1984
(ED2489011)

MacIntosh, Helen
SHARAF: The Canadian Shared Authority File Project.
Library Resources and Technical Services; v26 n4 p345-52 Oct-Dec 1982

Major-Database Disasters; Could They Happen Here?
American Libraries; v14 n10 p645-47 Nov 1983

Mann, Thomas W., Jr.; And Others
Library Automation: A Survey of Leading Academic and Public Libraries in the United States.
Peat, Marwick, Mitchell and Co., San Francisco, CA. 1986
(ED274369)

Martin, Susan K.
The New Technologies and Library Networks.
Library Journal; v109 n11 p1194-96 Jun 15 1984

Mason, Robert M.
Mason on Micros: EIDOS: Beyond Bibliographies.
Library Journal; v111 n18 p46-47 Nov 1 1986

McAninch, Glen
Bibliographic Utilities and the Use of Microcomputers in Libraries: Current and Projected Practices.
Microcomputers for Information Management: An International Journal for Library and Information Services; v3 n3 p217-31 Sep 1986

McCoy, Richard W.
The Linked Systems Project: Progress, Promise, Realities.
Library Journal; v111 n16 p33-39 Oct 1 1986

McKee, Elizabeth Chadbourn; Perry, Larry Stephen
Reference and OCLC: A Practical Checklist of Questions for the
Terminal.
RQ; v23 n3 p339-49 Spr 1984

Nasatir, Marilyn
Machine-Readable Data Files and Networks.
Information Technology and Libraries; v2 n2 p159-64 Jun 1983

Peel, Bruce; Kurmey, William J.
Cooperation among Ontario University Libraries.
Council of Ontario Universities, Toronto.
ISBN-0-88799-169-6
1983
Council of Ontario Universities, 130 St. George Street, Suite
8039, Toronto, ON, Canada M5S 2T4 ($3.00 per copy).
(ED233744)

Riedl, Richard
Computer Communications Potentials for Library Media Centers: An Introduction
School Library Media Activities Monthly; v3 n3 p28-31 Nov
1986

Rogers, JoAnn V.
Networking: Selected Research Studies, 1979-83.
Library and Information Science Research, An International
Journal; v6 n2 p111-32 Apr-Jun 1984

Rosen, Lynn M.; Owen, G.W. Brian
BCUC Data Base Loading and BCLN User and Data Base re-
quirements Study. BCUC Replication Study, Design Phase I.
Main Report.
British Columbia Union Catalogue, Richmond.
ISBN-0-919093-05-1
1981
(ED206310)

Schmidt, Karen A.; And Others
Technology at the Library of Congress.
Information Technology and Libraries v5 n4 p307-42 Dec 1986

Schultz, Lois
Bibliographic Utilities in the 1980's.
Library Hi Tech; v1 n3 p83-86 Win 1983

Schwarz, Philip J.
Management Decisions and the COM Catalog.
Microform Review; v11 n3 p156-71 Sum 1982

Senzig, Donna M.; Bright, Franklyn F.
The Network Library System: The History and Description of
an Evolving Library-Developed System.

Shoffer, Ralph M.; Madden, Mary A.
British Columbia Network: A Study of Feasibility.
Revised.
British Columbia Union Catalogue, Richmond.
ISBN-0-919093-00-0
1980
(ED200203)

Smalley, Donald A.; and Others
Linking the Bibliographic Utilities: Benefits and Costs.
Technical Report.
Council of Library Resources, Inc., Washington D.C.
1980
(ED195276)

Smith, Mary K.; and Others
Factors Shaping Library Systems in the 1980's; Trends in Net-
working, Part I; Part II.
Public Libraries; v25 n4 p126-29 Win 1986

Smith, Stephen H.
BCLN Hardware and Computing Facilities Evaluation Study.
Final Report.
British Columbia Union Catalogue, Richmond.
ISBN-0-919093-06-X

1981
(ED206309)

Steele, Colin; And Others
Communications.
Information Technology and Libraries; v5 n3 p228-42 Sep 1986

Sugnet, Chris, Ed.
Standards: Where Are We Headed? A Forum.
Library Hi Tech; v4 n2 p95-103 Sum 1986

Thompson, Dorothea M.
OCLC—A Personal Network.
RQ; v24 n3 p327-32 Spr 1985

Tillett, Barbara B.
1984 Automated Authority Control Opinion Poll: A Preliminary
Analysis.
Information Technology and Libraries; v4 n2 p171-78 Jun 1985

Turock, Betty J.; Turock, David L.
An Investigation of Public Library Participation in Biblio-
graphic Networks: Perceptions, Reactions, and Recommenda-
tions.
Library Resources and Technical Services; v31 n1 p35-59 Jan-
Mar 1987

Turner, Ann; And Others
DOBIS-WLN Impact Study Report.
British Columbia Union Catalogue, Richmond.
ISBN-0-919093-02-7
1980
(ED200205)

Wajenberg, Arnold; Gorman, Michael
OCLC's Database Conversion: A User's Perspective.
Journal of Library Automation; v14 n3 p174-89 Sep 1981

Watkins, Deane
Record Conversion at Oregon State.
Wilson Library Bulletin; v60 n4 p31-33 Dec 1985

Webster, Duane E.; Maruyama, Lenore S.
Ownership and Distribution of Bibliographic Data: Highlights
of a Meeting Held by the Library of Congress Network Advi-
sory Committee (March 4-5, 1980). Working Document.
Library of Congress, Washington D.C. Network Development
Office.
1980
(ED206293)

Webster, James K.; Warden, Carolyn L.
Comparing the Bibliographic Utilities for Special Librarians.
Special Libraries; v71 n12 p519-22 Dec 1980

Webster, James K.; Coty, Patricia A.
The S.L.A. Networking Committee.
Education Libraries; v7 n1-2 p25-28 Spr-Sum 1982

Index

DATE DUE
